En

The Apostle Paul had epic adventures following the Lord. Once, he ended up before a group of religious leaders fighting over his ancestry. The fight became so intense the commander feared they would tear Paul apart. Paul barely escaped the fight with his life. Later that night, the Lord stood by him and talked to him. The content of the conversation is revealing! He said, "You must testify (share your story) in Rome." There is real power in a life story! The story is power for the teller and transformational for the listener. For Paul, his story changed the world, saved lives, and shaped destinies.

My friend and one of our church leaders, Kelli Pharo, has penned a masterpiece story. You'll laugh, you'll cry, you'll cheer, and find yourself challenged as you journey with Kelli through an incredible life adventure. An adventure that reveals a powerful God-ordained purpose in Kelli! When you finish this book, I promise you won't be the same! It's highly possible that you will have discovered something that shapes your Field of Calling! The Apostle Paul's story did that for some terrified sailors in a broken ship. Kelli's story will do the same for you. The reader's life will be changed and their destiny shaped. Well done KP!! Ten thumbs up!!!

Kevin Craig
Senior Pastor
Thrive Church Apopka

I have always loved epic movies, it seems that they cannot only pull me into the story, but more importantly they move me by creating deep feelings and thought. *Fields of Calling* is such a book. It literally made me feel like I was on the front porch of a peaceful farmhouse listening to Kelli Pharo tell her story, but with me and my own life in mind. That's really what this book is all about. It's all about Kelli's story and how it can help you uncover and live out your own unique story. If you need someone to talk to you and to tell you a story, one that will help you in your own journey in this life, then you should read this book. Stories are the way we make sense of things, and Kelli's story is destined to help a lot of people find God's story for their life. Great book!

Donald Newman
Executive Director of Publishing
Salem Author Services

I remember so well watching Kelli stroll her daughter down the street of the neighborhood where we both lived at the time. We didn't know each other even though she lived only a few houses down from me and attended the same church. A few years later Kelli asked if we could meet over coffee, and there our friendship began. I have treasured our many conversations though the years. Kelli's book *Fields of Calling* shares her journey through life and pursuit to know God. I love how she is continually listening to hear God speak to her through objects, nature, dreams, numbers, His Word, and the voice of others. She has learned that pressing through life's challenges and difficulties is often necessary to accomplish destiny. You will be motivated by Kelli's stories to keep dreaming with God and to keep pursing all He has destined for you. Kelli is always up to a challenging conversation on hearing what God is currently saying and chasing His dreams. Grab a cup of coffee and *Fields of Calling* and let her inspire you to do the same.

Vickie Lewis
Health Care Administrator

FIELDS OF Calling

KELLI L. PHARO

FIELDS
OF *Calling*

Find Your Destiny; Fulfill Your Purpose

XULON PRESS

Xulon Press
2301 Lucien Way #415
Maitland, FL 32751
407.339.4217
www.xulonpress.com

Paperback ISBN-13: 978-1-6628-1800-4
Ebook ISBN-13: 978-1-6628-1801-1

Table of Contents

Introduction

HIS EYES MOVED around the room, going face to face, calling names, as he introduced the sales team that was typically on the road full-time to the office and warehouse staff that provided customer service and filled the medical device orders.

I was the youngest in the room at just twenty years old. He was probably the oldest, somewhere in his fifties. Branch managers have to be the oldest, don't they? It seems that way when you're just twenty.

He had almost completed the circuit, introducing each employee. Then his eyes met mine; and the name-calling stopped. It seemed that he paused for an eternity, though it was probably only ten seconds. He knew he knew me. I worked for him. But he had a big office, and I wandered the warehouse with a rolling cart. He was on his second wife, lived in a big house, and had a new Scottish Terrier puppy. I lived with my parents and drove a pickup truck with no power steering or air conditioning. Ten seconds is an eternity when you're the only one in the room your branch manager can't remember.

Finally, he spoke. "All I can think of is Kitten," he said. Laughter from the sales, office, and warehouse staff. *Kitten? That's all he could think of?* Well, my name is Kelli. So, I guess he got some of the important letters right. But how humiliating. *My fifty-year-old, Scottie-daddy, big-house, second-wife branch manager just called me Kitten, in front of a few dozen fellow employees. What do I do? They're laughing at me!*

I quickly collected my thoughts. "Simon," I said. "I told you not to call me that at work." Roaring laughter came from the sales, office, and warehouse staff. I won! I deflected! I was clever! No one was thinking about how I was the forgotten one now; I was the funny one instead.

Thirty-plus years have gone by since the Kitten incident. Now I'm the manager in my fifties, with a big house, a second spouse, and a Pomeranian puppy. How did this happen? How did I get here? I'm not that insecure, young, forgotten one any longer. But I did learn something important that day that I've carried with me over the years.

Everyone wants to be remembered. Everyone wants to be heard. Everyone has value. Everyone has a destiny.

I hold no grudge from that incident with the branch manager from years ago. He had a momentary lapse in memory; or, maybe he really just didn't know me well. Either way, his forgetting my name doesn't mean I'm not important or that I don't matter. But it's taken me a lifetime, and many more incidents similar to the Kitten incident, to help me realize my value; and that maybe, just maybe, the tough times are just as important to my destiny as the good times are.

When I was younger, I did not realize that I had a destiny. I knew I liked certain things and hoped for certain outcomes, but I did not realize that these desires were placed within me by my Creator. My love for horses, my ability to lead, the skills I have as a communicator, and my passion to see others succeed—they are all part of what I'm called to. My calling, my destiny, my testimony is mine alone. Nobody else could have walked in my shoes, because God created me to walk this path. And the same is true for you. The stories you could tell, what you're interested in, how you process things, the skills you have—all part of your individual calling. You are a part of God's plan. Your role matters. You matter. No one else can do what you are called to do.

So if, like me, you have questioned who you are, why you were created, and what your purpose is—in vocation, education, ministry—the stories I share in this book will encourage you to examine your life with fresh eyes and discover answers to these questions for yourself. You just need to know what to look for and how to interpret what you find. Join me as I share my journey of destiny discovered: a journey to find my voice, to discover my purpose, and to enter my field of calling.

CHAPTER 1:
You Have a Destiny

*"Extraordinary things only happen to extraordinary people.
Maybe it's a sign that you've got an extraordinary destiny—
something greater than you could have imagined."*
The Voyage of the Dawn Treader *by C.S. Lewis*

IT WAS 1970, the year before the gates of Orlando's Disney World opened for the first time, when right up the road from Magic Kingdom, my family and I moved to the little suburb of Pine Hills, Florida. I was three years old and shared a room with my sister, where we had white twin beds and a nightstand in-between.

At different points along the next fifteen years, we'd put a swing set in the backyard, plant annual gardens that only seemed to produce radishes and nothing else, erect a storage shed that I dreamt would be a barn for my future dream horse, and knocked out the dining room window to add a flat-roofed family room on the back of that little house.

Just beyond the cul-de-sac where our home sat was an orange grove; it became the hub of our childhood exploits. Neighborhood ball games were a regular activity in the sand lot that fronted that orange grove. My young friends and I spent our days roller skating, riding bikes, and playing in the dirt. The older, cooler kids skateboarded and listened to albums. It was the 1970s: we had Farrah-Fawcett-feathered hair, bell bottoms, and tube socks. Most days, we stayed outside until dark or skinned knees brought us in to Mom and Dad.

The youngest of four, I was the least of these. I had no particular talent; I was not a beautiful child. Nothing about me said, "This kid's going places." But as I look back at my Pine Hills childhood and beyond, I can see that God was preparing me. He was teaching me. He was stretching me so that I could walk in my gifts on my path of destiny. And I can assure you that as you take stock of your life, you'll see the times He was doing the same for you. Because every life has a destiny; I believe it to my core.

This is a book about destiny. It is my story, my testimony. We all have a testimony that holds truth and revelation for others. There is power in our testimonies. Revelation 12:11 says that we overcome the enemy by the blood of the Lamb, but also by our testimony.

My story may have begun in a sweet, little suburb growing radishes by an orange grove, but it's so much more. My story is of a child learning to be prophetic and an intercessor long before knowing what these meant. The story of being a horse-crazy kid that never outgrew her equine obsession. The story of enduring years of abuse because of a misinformed view of God's call to faithfulness. The story of restoration, retribution, and realization of inner strength: and the call to do justice, love mercy, and walk humbly.

I'll come back to that. But first, I've identified some questions to get us thinking. As we go along, it will be helpful for you to ask yourself these questions and make note of your responses.

What do you like or need to make you happy?

I like people. But I also need time alone; especially early in the morning, when the world is still and quiet. I like trees, and land, and nature. Sitting and looking out at the grass and trees, hearing the birds sing fills me with peace. I like animals, but especially horses. Their beauty is mesmerizing, and interacting with them is fun. I like corporate worship and learning about the Word of God. I like serving. I like leading. I like revelation, and I find it even sweeter when I have to drill down and study in the process of discovery. I like reading, writing, teaching, and instructing. I find understanding, knowledge, and wisdom so precious when they come. I get jazzed up sharing with others what I learn. I like home décor, decorating, shopping, and watching HGTV. I like a clean house, a well-weeded planter bed, and organization. I like to encourage people and see them succeed, especially my children. Their smiles and laughter are what I like most.

So, now what? This brief inventory is all about what I like and what makes me happy. Can you make a similar list? What do we do with these lists? There are clues in our lists that point to our created purposes.

Though there is some debate about who said the following, it is sage advice: "Find a job you enjoy doing, and you will never have to work a day in your life." (Popik)

No matter who said it, I think what that person meant was that in loving what you're doing, the work is more pleasurable. It's not only good advice; it is also how God created you.

While pleasure should not be the sole impetus for a career choice, in order to do a job well, we should be in favor of what we are doing and do it with all our creative might. God set this example in His Word.

Genesis 1 opens the Bible with a God who is doing two things: creating and working. Over and over, when He completes a step of His creative work, He steps back and sees that it is good. Much like painters or sculptors would do when creating a piece of art: they step back, look at what they did, and find pleasure in personal success.

When we realize what drives us, what brings us satisfaction, what is within us to do, it is fulfilling, and we want to continue to do that thing. This is what work is meant to be.

Thinking about the things that make you happy can point you to that at which you'll be successful, because it points you to your personal creativity, and it points you to what your fulfilling efforts may look like.

Do you like to be inside air-conditioning where it's clean and comfortable, or do you like to be outside, getting your hands dirty? Do you like quiet work spaces, or does a lot of action and sound inspire you? Perhaps you are a morning person or a night owl. Achieving small tasks or large goals may motivate you.

Paying attention to what you like and what's important to you is recognizing that God created you uniquely.

Along these lines, I highly recommend the book *The 5 Love Languages* by Gary Chapman. Knowing what fills your tank and then pursuing a calling that aligns will help keep you going, even when things are tough.

My primary love language seems to have shifted over time. For years, it was words of encouragement, but I find acts of service float my boat too. When I interviewed for my current job, I communicated to the CEO that if I was not encouraged verbally from time to time, I would not be a happy employee. This is important information to have. And now, in a position of leadership within my organization, I have each of my employees take a love language test so that I know what motivates them. I want to speak their language and fill their tanks, just as I want this for myself.

What have you always wanted to do?

I had five childhood dreams for my life. I wanted to own a horse, I wanted some land, I wanted a career as a horse-racing jockey, I wanted to adopt children internationally, and I wanted to be a missionary.

I'll let you in on a secret: We don't get everything we want. Because sometimes, we are not created for certain paths.

And what we think we want may not be a fully mature picture of what we were created for.

I am five feet, ten inches tall. I did not become a jockey, but I am in a career that centers around horses, which is what I believe was the impetus for that childish desire.

The other four dreams I had as a child have come true. I have owned several horses over the years. I do live on a couple acres of land. I did adopt my children internationally. And while the mission field does not look like I imagined, I would call myself a missionary.

I'll let you in on a secret: We don't get everything we want. Because sometimes, we are not created for certain paths. And what we think we want may not be a fully mature picture of what we were created for.

My love of missionaries and the work they do came from my childhood experiences growing up in Lockhart Methodist Church, in Lockhart, Florida.

Somehow, our church had gotten connected with a musical group under the leadership of Terry Law, out of Oral

Roberts University. This group of singing students called themselves Living Sound. And they toured the world, spreading the gospel through song. It was the 1970s, so the music was groovy and so were they. And when they went places like the Soviet Europe, known as the Iron Curtain at that time, they were often invited in as a rock 'n' roll band. But their music touched people's hearts, and their impact was deep and wide.

Each year, at some point during their tour season, they would end up at our little church. We would host the band members in our homes and provide them a weeklong respite, including trips to Disney and much-needed down time.

We always looked forward to those visits. I still remember my mom cleaning and preparing for days before their arrival—we typically hosted one of the group's married couples in our home. And in the evenings, after one of their concerts, we'd all sit around the kitchen table, eating and visiting. I remember thinking how lucky I was to be hanging out with world-traveling musicians in my home!

I really admired that group of young adults for the work they did for the kingdom, and I hung on every word of their stories about their ministry adventures. It truly had a deep impact on my walk with God and my call to spread the gospel.

I believe today that my everyday life, the territory I live in, and the job I do are my mission fields.

That territory is a small city in Central Florida, where I live with my husband, Chris, and two of our kids.

Apopka, from the Native American "Ahapopka," or "potato eating place," is a lovely, little community on the north-western corner of Orlando. We love this city; and we know that God called our family here.

My childhood home in Pine Hills is just ten miles outside of Apopka. And when Chris and I married and looked for a place to raise a family, we felt led to Apopka.

We've lived here nineteen years now, and we've been a part of the same church all these years—Thrive Church Apopka. We love serving there, shoulder to shoulder with our many friends. Our pastor, Kevin Craig, is an incredibly anointed man. He is used mightily by God, yet remains a humble, loving leader.

When God called us to this place, it wasn't just to have a home and put down roots. The desire for a close community where our kids could go to school with their friends from church was real. But God had a bigger call on our place in this city.

Apopka is our territory. I feel personally responsible for praying over the people that live here. And I regularly list off the names of the streets throughout our city, praying over the residents that live along those streets and within the city borders and beyond.

Sometimes, I drive through the areas where poverty and crime have too often found homes among many loving, good people. I care for these people. I pray blessings over them. I bind the movement of drugs and drug addiction within our city. I pray protection over the children walking to school, the law enforcement officers protecting and serving, and the many churches and businesses among us.

It's my responsibility to cover my city in prayer. And within this territory, I have power and authority to do so. It's my territory. God gave it to me. This is my mission field.

Where we live is important, but so too is what we do where we live.

What about you? What area do you feel called to? Perhaps you have a call to travel. Maybe you've got a book inside you. Or, there might be a foreign language you wish you could master. Starting a new business may seem exciting to you. Whatever has been pulling at you—that thing you can't seem to forget or ignore—that might be pointing you to your calling.

My love for horses has been lifelong. Even as a child, I felt the tug to have a career that revolved around horses. But it wasn't until I was in my forties that the vision began to crystalize into what that might look like. ·

I have always worked hard. As a kid, I'd ask my mom if I could wash the windows or do other tasks around the house. In high school, I had three jobs. I worked several days a week for TG&Y, a retail home goods and clothing store. One day a week, I worked at a small western wear store. And occasionally I worked for a local barn, caring for the horses whenever the owner was away at a horse show. In college, I also worked three jobs—in an internship with a software firm; running the computer lab at my college; and a couple times a week at a local show barn: cleaning stalls, caring for horses, and tacking up lesson horses.

Right out of high school, I had a job working for a thoroughbred race training barn. And today, in my fifties, I'm part of the executive team leading a nonprofit that serves people with trauma and those with cognitive or physical disabilities through horses. In the years between these horse-centered jobs, I've owned horses, taken riding lessons, gotten certified in a couple of equine-centered skills, and read a lot about horses. But even though horses are one of my passions, I have not focused solely on horse skills. I completed a college education in writing, volunteered in areas where I could serve and lead people, studied the Bible, read

Christian literature, and attended workshops to build various skills. Because I know that in order to fulfill my destiny and glorify God in my work, I need to not just be a horse person; I need to be a knowledgeable business person, a skilled professional, and a humble servant leader.

I don't know for sure what else lies in my career path, or what other areas I'll go into as part of my life's walk. But I do try to always stay open to a winding path of destiny.

What do you believe you do well?

For many years, I would jokingly say, "Someday, someone is going to pay me to ride my own horse." It was, of course, my jovial way of saying that the dream is to do for a career what I loved to do for recreation. But a couple of years ago, I was exercising a horse at the barn where I work when it suddenly occurred to me that I was riding a horse that everyone referred to as "Kelli's horse." I was being paid to ride "my own horse"! I get a kick out of realizing that, just as the Scriptures say, life and death truly are in the power of the tongue.

I love horses, but I didn't decide to love horses. It's part of who I am and part of my destiny.

I also like to write and to study. I enjoy quiet time alone as much as I enjoy times of deep conversation with others. Again, all part of my spiritual DNA.

I've heard that for many people, speaking in public is a fate worse than death. I cannot imagine this; I love speaking in public. Sometimes, it's easier to talk to thousands than it is to talk to one.

I didn't develop this ability by doing Toastmasters. Though I believe that is a valuable organization for teaching the skills of public speaking. I grew into it. God put within me the ability to bravely speak in public, and to speak effectively. Even in elementary school, I was often the emcee for student events held in an auditorium full of people. I loved to entertain the crowds freestyle.

Public speaking is part of my spiritual DNA.

I also have the gift of counsel. I did not develop it on my own; it came with the decision to pursue humility. And I was not the one that identified it within myself. It's been called upon by other leaders in my life and has opened doors of opportunity and forged relationships.

I'm a planner and an organizer. I love bringing order from chaos. I love thinking strategically and doing long-term planning.

So, what do I do with my abilities to speak, write, counsel, plan, organize, strategize, and work with horses? I could do nothing. That's my choice. But within me is a destiny to use these specific traits to walk a certain path; all placed within me by my Creator. It's taken me a lifetime to pull all these things together into what I believe is the path for my life. But I think I'm on the right track. I'm beginning to see a plan.

Things you like, things you're good at, things that come naturally, and things that interest you may all be signposts to your calling.

God told the prophet Jeremiah that He created him for a purpose. "*Before I formed you in the womb I knew you, before you were born I set you apart; I appointed you as a prophet to the nations*" (Jer. 1:5, NIV). God actually gave Jeremiah a job assignment before he was even born!

Being created with a destiny and a calling does not mean that we do not have choices. We absolutely do. In fact, God instructs us to "*choose you this day whom ye will serve*" (Josh. 24:15, KJV). He actually tells us in the sixteenth chapter of Proverbs that it's a partnership between Him and us. "*Commit to the Lord whatever you do, and He will establish your plans*" (v. 3, NIV), and "*In their hearts humans plan their course, but the Lord establishes their steps*" (v. 9, NIV).

We are born with a purpose and a destiny. We make the decisions how to go after what drives us. And when we decide what we want, the Lord orders our steps to achieve it.

At all times, God is in your corner, waiting to partner with you on your journey. The choices you make can align you for one path or another. Staying in communion with Him is essential to being aware of sign posts, markers, and supplies along the way.

Do you feel you have a mission? What causes these strong pulls within us to set off down certain paths? It's our spiritual DNA: our gifts, talents, and desires.

You can easily recognize your spiritual DNA by asking yourself some questions, but you can also recognize it by listening to what others say about you, which brings us to the next question.

What do other people tell you you're good at?

Have others recognized certain gifts in you? Often, other people see the gifts within us better than we see them ourselves. If more than one person has mentioned that he or she recognizes certain things in you, it could be a clue. Someone might tell you that you are intuitive, well-spoken, kind-hearted, a talented speaker, good with kids, artistic, etc. Listen for repeated recognition from others. And if it rings true in your gut, it's a clue.

Have you seen promotion in an area? Promotion can look like a variety of things. Your pastor may ask you to lead a Bible study because he recognizes your teaching gift. Your child's teacher may ask if you can participate as a class mom because she recognizes your gift of helping. Or, you might be promoted at work because you show promise in your career. In what areas are those in authority calling on you?

Do your promotions align with your interests? This is a good checkpoint for promotion. If you are called on to take responsibility, does it line up with what you are interested in? If it does, even indirectly, it might be a clue.

I have been complemented on my writing, my speaking, my counseling, and my decorating abilities. The first three talents help me in my job regularly, as well as in my relationships and serving in the church. The ability to decorate my home nicely may not guide my career decisions, but it's a fun hobby; and it helps me to understand myself as creative.

My husband, Chris, and I have renovated three fixer-uppers over the years. We loved living in each of them and were happy with the results. In 2019, we purchased what will most likely be our last big project; it was a total overhaul.

For various reasons, this time, we hired a contractor for the renovations.

When we first walked into the forty-year-old abandoned house, in my mind, I could see the new kitchen, the moved walls, the furniture placement. But I could also see on the faces of friends and family that they could not see what I saw was possible. Today, with all the work done and all the furniture and décor in place, they understand my vision.

Perhaps I could have made this talent a career. I think God gives us options. We get to choose! But God also gave me a lot of other skills that work well in my current career. And I love that I have a hobby that interests me; it's my creative outlet.

When we were still somewhat new to our church, there was a gentleman who was into dream interpretation, and it kind of freaked me out. I really didn't want anything to do with it.

Several years later, our pastor invited prophetic speaker, author, and coach Doug Addison to come speak at our church and to conduct a class on dreams. I was unfamiliar with who Doug was at that time. But I went because I trust my pastor, even though I still thought it was odd. I was, after all, a lifetime dreamer.

During the class, Doug made dreams and understanding dreams less weird and more sensible. I came to understand that God speaking to us through our dreams is scriptural and very much for our benefit. I wasn't sold on it by the end of the class, but I felt better about it.

When the class ended, our pastor was thanking Doug for teaching us when he announced to those of us in attendance that our church was going to take what Doug had taught us and start a class on dream interpretation for our members. Then he announced that I was going to be the one to teach it.

What?! Me?!

I have to tell you that my pastor is an incredibly godly, humble, prophetic leader, and I know he was speaking what God was telling him that day. It was shocking news to me, but it was accurate.

Because I trust my pastor, and in order to honor him and what God had told him, I went all in. I read everything I could about dream interpretation. Doug, and others, have some incredible, Bible-based resources on this topic.

I also began journaling my dreams and practicing interpretation on my own dreams. But mostly, I studied the Word of God and asked the Holy Spirit for insight.

That was the year God began to speak to me in incredible ways, and deep revelation was released to me in my dreams and in other ways. Once I opened up and humbled myself, God had permission to speak. I was ready to listen.

I did teach those classes for my church—just as my pastor had declared. And I think I benefited more than anyone.

This experience also helped me to discover my leadership calling. I'll share more on that later, but I highly recommend Arthur A. Burk's book *The Redemptive Gifts of Individuals*. This in-depth look at the seven redemptive gifts found in Romans 12:6-7 will help you discover more about yourself and why you may be good at certain things.

What do you not like or what's not important to you?

Not a morning person? Then you may not be called to be a farmer or a school bus driver. Knowing what you don't like can help you discover what you're not called to do.

I worked several jobs between high school and college. And I figured out I did not want to work weekends. So, I looked for a career that was Monday-Friday for the most part. I also learned that I did not want to serve food or sell things.

When I was just out of high school, I took my teenage dream job. I went to work for a thoroughbred race training barn. It was probably the most fun I've ever had on a job. I came to work early in the morning to help care for a barn full of two-year-old thoroughbred horses that were in training to become racehorses. The other grooms and I cleaned stalls, fed the horses, turned them in and out, bathed them, applied leg wraps, and hot-walked them. The exercise riders took them around the track, taught them to break from a starting gate, and conditioned them to be their best and fastest.

At the end of the day, we took turns driving the tractor out to the orange groves that were part of the couple hundred acres that made up the farm. Behind the tractor was a trailer load of everything that had been picked out of the stalls that day. The tractor driver was also the "manure distributor." Drive a little forward and stop, climb in back, scoop a shovel load of manure, and fling it hard enough that it is distributed across the ground. Drive a little forward, and do it again, over and over, until the trailer was empty.

I still remember the days when it was my turn to take the manure out to spread. Even on rainy days, as I got soaked to the bone in a downpour, I'd sing a happy tune as I drove that tractor and spread that manure. I was so fulfilled by that job, working with horses, even if it meant slinging manure in the rain. I was learning a little more every day. I was even in training to be an exercise rider.

Although I loved the job, track life is a hard life. We worked six days a week, for about ten hours a day. And ultimately, it was the weekend work that was causing me to miss church and made me realize it was not the right job for me. It was not a bad experience. I loved it! But it opened my eyes to what was important to me.

What would you do if money was no object?

Do you have something you'd like to design, patent, and sell? Maybe you'd like to start a company or a nonprofit. Or, maybe going to college is your dream yet to be fulfilled.

My heart's desire is to start a nonprofit here in Apopka that serves people through horses. Like helping kids learn to read by doing story time with horses; or providing a space where elderly people with dementia can interact with horses—studies are showing great promise in this area—or doing mental health work with people using horses. There are so many incredible ways horses help people!

What's your dream? Do you think about something often? Perhaps you journal ideas or talk them over with friends. Your heart's desire, unhampered by budgetary limits, could be a clue to your calling.

Now that you've considered what you like, what you're good at, and what you don't like or are not good at, in the next chapter, we'll look at the battles we face on our journeys. What types of resistance have you encountered?

We all experience difficulties. And often, we mistake hard times as setbacks to our walk. What we discover through God's Word is that He uses the hard things to knock off the rough edges.

CHAPTER 2:
The Early Years

❦

"Before we were even born, He gave us our destiny; that we would fulfill the plan of God who always accomplishes every purpose and plan in his heart." Ephesians 1:11 (TPT)

I'VE HAD ENCOUNTERS with God throughout my life. Even as a small child, I experienced God in big ways. And I believe that as a child, my spiritual DNA was being developed.

My kindergarten class party looked like it could be a bust. Whoever was responsible for the drinks did not plan well.

We had just one can of purple juice for an entire class of five-year-olds and the parents who came to help.

Having just learned the story of Jesus performing His first miracle of multiplying wine at the wedding feast, I prayed over that grape-flavored juice with childlike faith. And God heard that prayer, multiplying the juice. That one small can served twenty to thirty thirsty people. God was building my faith.

When I was about twelve, my sister and I were in her room playing with a deck of cards. She would hold up a card, and I would guess what card she was holding. Each time she held up a card, I would think deep within myself before guessing the card. And time after time, I got it right. It freaked me out, and I stopped the game.

For years, I thought this was the enemy trying to manipulate me and twist the power of God speaking in my life. I only just recently realized it was God teaching me to have ears to hear; to connect with the Holy Spirit within me.

It was not important that I could "guess" what card was being held up. It was important that I tapped into my ability to look deep into the Spirit for understanding. God was sharpening my hearing.

Can you think of times when your own faith was stretched and tested? Was God preparing you for the walk He's called you to?

I am very blessed to have godly parents who raised my siblings and me in church. They taught Sunday school, helped at church events, carted youth around to outings, and my dad even filled in when the preacher was gone, delivering the sermon in his absence.

My parents also took us to crusades. I look back in gratitude at having been part of packed-out auditoriums, listening to such greats as Kathryn Kuhlman and Billy Graham.

The effort and commitment that my parents put into the lives of my siblings and me has a great deal to do with our individual faith walks to this day. But even though God was developing my gifts and my character in those early years, the enemy was working on me too.

What types of resistance have you encountered?

Are you experiencing resistance in an area? Often, when we know what we like and where we want to go, we find ourselves blocked from progressing as we keep hitting up against walls. The enemy always wants to thwart our growth and promotion. But there are also times when God allows roadblocks to slow us down or divert us for our own good.

If you encounter a block on your path or if you are faced with a big decision, it's a wise first step to seek counsel. This may come through prayer and the Word of God, or it may come through counsel with those in your life who have godly wisdom. For big decisions, get several confirmations before taking action.

We have an enemy that does not want us to fulfill our potential. So, it's natural that you'll come up against resistance at some point as you track toward your calling. It takes spiritual wisdom to know if obstacles you encounter are roadblocks to protect you from taking the wrong route or resistance that the enemy is bringing to impede your success. This, again, is why communion with the Holy Spirit is vital to our daily walks. He is our guide, our companion, and our friend. It's important to spend time with Him daily, getting to know His voice and His ways.

It takes spiritual wisdom to know if obstacles you encounter are roadblocks to protect you from taking the wrong route or resistance that the enemy is bringing to impede your success.

I was listening to a podcast this morning on my way into work, as I do most days. This one was by Prophet James Goll. I just love his fatherly insight and revelation.

He was interviewing musician Danny Gokey. And Danny said something that was so simple but so profound: "Truth does not transform, until it's truth received. And lies do not transform, until they are lies received." (Goll)

You can sit in church and hear the Word of God preached. But until you get it down inside you as truth, it will not change your life. God says He is good and He is righteous and just. He says He loves us and is available to counsel us and comfort us, build us up, prosper us, and so on. But you have to let it become truth in your life. Accepting God's Word as truth will cause you to move forward and upward.

And the same is true of the lies the enemy tries to feed us. He tells us it's hopeless, we'll never get out of this situation, we're not worthy, God is unjust, and so on. If we listen, if we entertain those thoughts, if we let those down inside us, they will transform us. But it will be a downward spiral.

We have to receive the truth of who God created us to be in order to continue to move forward. Resist the resistor and be encouraged by the encourager.

Often, the very area to which God is calling us is the part of life where we experience the greatest resistance. And it will take some warring to break through and gain ground.

Joseph was first sold into slavery and spent years in prison before being promoted and saving a nation. Moses was adopted, murdered a man, and argued with God before saving his people. Paul was killing Christians before God got his attention to spread the gospel.

I've had this conversation with so many people. We talk about how we realize there is a spiritual war going on around us, but we just don't really want to be a part of that fight. We'd rather live in victory without having to be victorious. But victory only comes after you've won a battle.

In fact, we are all called to war; it's just a part of the human-spiritual walk. But the good news is that we are equipped with God's armor, and when we show up and do our part, then He fights our battles for us. It's our job to hide in Him and let Him cover us with His wings.

The first few verses of Ephesians 6 tell us that we will have to wrestle against principalities, powers, and rulers of darkness. But that in order to do so, we'll need to put on the armor of God. And once we put on that armor, and once we've done everything that the crisis demands, we are to stand. When we stand and let God fight, we win the battle.

The resistance you encounter may be self-inflicted. I tell my kids all the time, who you are is determined by what you let in the gate—your eye gate, ear gate, and mouth gate. Let junk inside you, and you'll feel it. And you'll put junk out. But let in health, love, encouragement, godliness, and goodness, and you'll feel that. And that's what you'll put back out. Watch what you put before your eyes, ears, and mouth. And if you've made mistakes in the past, let God heal and forgive it. There is mercy for all.

Taking Authority

There are times when resistance is truly and blatantly from the enemy. And the good news is, as a child of God, He *"hath made us kings and priests"* (Rev. 1:6, KJV). This means we wear both the robe of power and the ring of authority. The enemy has power, yes; but under the blood of Jesus, he has no authority to use it at all. We have to recognize our rights and speak up for ourselves.

Something within me, placed in my nature by God, has a certain, stubborn authority in face of adversity: even when facing an angry Russian judge (I'll get to that shortly), and even when accosted by a woman under the influence of the enemy.

Out to dinner one evening years ago, I was sitting with my dinner date, enjoying my meal, when a woman entered the restaurant. There was obviously something not right about her. She wandered the aisle, going table by table, muttering and causing disruption. I knew she was coming for me before she even sat herself down on the bench next to me. And I was ready.

She slid in next to me and began a tirade of unintelligible accusations aimed in my direction. She was obviously being manipulated by the enemy, as she was attempting to exert power. But the Spirit within me rose up as I turned to her, looking her in her eyes, and firmly stating with authority, "You have to leave now!" She immediately stood up and quickly left the building.

We do not have to put up with the enemy's accusations, attacks, and lies. We are sons and daughters of the reigning king.

Unfortunately, sometimes it takes a difficult road for us to learn what the lies of the enemy look like. For me, learning my value and worth has been an uphill hike.

Rejected

At a young age, I learned low self-esteem. I was very skinny and awkward. I was not in possession of obvious talent or anything that set me apart as a child of worth and value—at least not in my own eyes. And I felt the sting of worthlessness often, as other kids spoke cruel words over me.

To make matters worse, I internalized the rejection, and it made me want to hide who I was. I didn't want to wear dresses or be girly, because my femininity was attacked. I did not struggle with gender identity; I just wanted to hide who I was because I felt I was not acceptable. I spent a lot of time alone the older I got.

As I matured along with my peers, their teenage bodies were beginning to become more womanly, but mine stayed skinny and gangly. I was so thin in my early teen years that my kneecaps were bigger-around than my thighs.

Girls who had been my playmates as children now shunned me and hid from me. Some of it was based on my awkwardness, I'm sure, but much of it was my relationship with God. I would not give in to the temptations that many of them wrestled with. I had chosen to follow the Lord at any cost; and there was a cost.

I remember a conversation with a friend my age and an older girl she emulated. This particular friend was one of the ones who had begun to shun me and refused me a seat next to her on the school bus the first day of junior high school. Somehow, the summer had become a dividing line. She was now on the cool side, and I had stayed behind the line.

During the conversation, she told me that the problem with me was that I was just "too straight." She was, of course, referring to my resistance to give in to worldly temptations. In my naivety, however, I assumed she was referring to my less-than-womanly figure. "Straight" meant flat-chested, in my mind. And so my response to her observation was, "Well, if I could do anything about it, don't you think I would?!"

Imagine the look of confusion on her face at my remark. Perhaps she was accurate in her assessment—I was "too straight."

Unfortunately, I did not learn this lesson quickly; you should move on from friends who want to move on from you. As later that year, I was jumped and beaten by three girls while defending that same friend. When the dust settled, she was nowhere to be found.

Fortunately, in my second year of junior high school, I had a change of scenery. Several of my friends from church and I began attending a private Christian school. I still struggled with self-love and dealt with the occasional belittling remark, but it was incredible to be in school with my best friends from church. Those gals are still my friends to this day.

The enemy wanted me to doubt my worth. But I know that I am worthy because my heavenly Father says that I am.

Through it all, as I transitioned from childhood to teen years and into my adult life, I never lost faith in God. And He was faithful to me. And though it has matured over the years, even back then I had an ear to hear God speak.

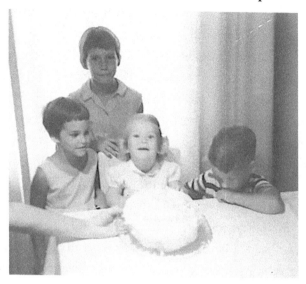

My First Birthday

Shame Off You

As I write this, it's my birthday weekend. I have always thought my birthdate was significant. And God speaks to me through the numbers of my birthday: 7/14/66. That's 77766: God's number and man's number in juxtaposition, right next to each other. I'm part of the plan God has to bring His love, His hope, and His salvation message to the world. I think we are all called to that. But for me, my birth-date is intentional; it is a confirmation to me personally.

Right before I was born, my mom was caught in a swarm of wasps that stung her multiple times. They were concerned that it could have an effect on me since she was so far along. I turned out fine, but I believe it was an attack of the enemy on my life from the beginning. I'm a threat. (And so are you!) And I intend to remain a threat. Only I intend to go beyond just being a threat; I am an undefeatable foe to the enemy, by the blood and name of Jesus. I have all authority and power given to me as a child of the King. I am a priest and a king because He gave me His robe and His ring. And I have authority to command that the enemy has no power over anything within my realm, my territory. I reign with the Lord here. My words carry authority, and I speak peace, protection, joy, hope, love, and forward movement over my family, our health, our home, our bank account, our jobs, our church, our community, our city, etc. And my words have authority to remove rejection from my life.

If you've ever had the phrase "shame on you" spoken over you, or you have spoken it over others, undo that harm. Nobody needs shame spoken onto them. Break that curse and speak, "Shame off you." That's what the blood of Jesus does for us; it removes the shame and the stain.

Speaking positive, life-giving words does not mean we won't have any difficulties. We all have to battle for what's ours. And battles have ups and downs. We just have to keep moving forward. No retreat!

Then Came Marriage

When I was twenty years old, I married a man that professed to love the Lord. Before our engagement, I sought counsel in the decision, and I had my parents' blessing. People in his life spoke over him as well, that I was the wife for him. But not long into our ten-year marriage, it became obvious that my young husband had not overcome the difficulties of his life: and it was affecting his behavior, his beliefs, and the way he treated me. I endured a difficult and, many times, abusive marriage.

I would not leave because I thought God would not want me to be divorced. And I did not speak up and tell anyone what I was going through because I'd been taught that wives were not to speak badly about their husbands. So, I prayed, I endured, and I suffered.

Before I continue, I want to interject a very clear message. Please understand that I did not handle my situation correctly. No one should suffer abuse. Faithfulness does not mean you should remain silent if you are being victimized. I should have sought help. Protecting yourself does not mean you are not faithful. If you are with a partner who harms you, you should seek safety and help.

And I also want to interject this—before you commit to being with someone for life, you should find opportunities to see him or her at his or her best and at his or her worst. You need to understand how the person reacts when things don't go his or her way. And you should pay attention to how that person treats other people—parents, strangers, people in authority, the down and out. This will give you a glimpse into how the person will treat you when infatuation wears off and real life begins.

I remember at some point in our marriage, we were attending a couple's Sunday school class. And the pastor was making the point that if he had to do all over again, he'd marry his wife. He went so far as to ask those of us in the class to indicate that we'd do the same. What an internal struggle! I would NOT marry the man I had married if given the chance to do so again; I would not divorce him either. But what a tortuous thought to have presented—a chance to escape pending pain and torment. I could not reveal my thoughts, and I'm sure the pastor had no indication that anyone in the room would be as conflicted as I was. But it haunted me. I could not be untrue, but I could not embarrass my husband by being truthful. I did my best to avoid being part of the response. I sat quietly. I sat in misery.

Ten years of mental and physical harm: Then he divorced me when he'd had enough of me and wanted to move on to other women.

In that time, I had just lost our unborn child, and now I'd lost a husband, my home, many of my possessions, my pets, my church, most of my friends, and a lot of hope. We had been quite active in our church. In fact, we helped to found it. But when my husband told me he wanted a divorce, I left in shame. I moved back to my parents' home about an hour away.

Here's my message to the church: It is not our job to judge anyone. It is our job to love.

Following years of serving and worshipping in that church of hundreds, only two people extended the love of God to me when my husband and I split. One was an elderly saint who checked on me a few times to make sure I was okay. And the other was my friend and member of the small home group that met in our house.

I'm not sharing this to shame anyone or to say that I have unforgiveness, because I hold no grudge. After all, I was the one who moved away in shame. But it has opened my eyes to my own lack of care for those who are hurting. It's not my place to judge. I am the hands and heart of Jesus. I must love.

The thing about shame and rejection and worry is that they will not let you rest. And during that difficult time, I slept very little. I averaged about an hour or two a night. And what sleep I did get was not restful. I lay awake mourning loss and fretting over the future.

I was thirty years old. My plans for a marriage, home, and children had all been swallowed up in a big, black hole. I was alone, I had no plans for a way forward, and I had never told anyone about the abuse I'd been through in the previous ten years. It would be another seven years before I would begin to open up about that.

Several weeks after our split, as I was in prayer one night, the Lord told me to turn to Proverbs 19:23 (NASB). I had no idea what the verse was about, but I turned to it immediately.

> *"The fear of the Lord leads to life,*
> *so that one may sleep satisfied, untouched by evil."*

I read that verse, and deep within me, I felt its truth. I went to sleep and slept eight hours. From that point forward, I slept soundly each night. That verse became life to me. And it set me on a study of what it means to fear the Lord—to be aware of His goodness and His might with respect and awe.

I know that there is life and power in the living Word of God because I've seen it in my life.

Because of the struggles of some of my siblings, and my own abusive marriage, there was a lot of trauma and upheaval in my life from twelve to thirty. But through it all, God was with me. And I never lost hope or trust. An eternal optimist, I'm always expecting something good is just around the corner.

My Husband, Children, and Me, 2010

The Pharo Five, 2019

What has God said?

What has God said? This is, of course, the most important question we should seek out with the most intent. Have you asked God what your assignment is? Working in partnership with the Holy Spirit is key to discovering the answer to all the questions of calling.

There are many ways to hear from God, but you must be ready to listen. A quiet mind, a dedicated time, an attitude of humility all prepare us to listen for God's voice. It comes in sounds, in impressions, through the Word of God, through symbols and signs, through numbers, in words from others.

If you feel your call is large or heavy, you may need to get extra confirmation. Spending time in fasting and prayer is always wise in these times. And counseling with your pastor or others who speak authoritatively into your life is a good idea.

I try to never make big decisions quickly. And I saw the fruit of not taking time to heed wisdom when we put in a pool at our house a few years back.

Chris and I had promised our kids that when we moved into a new house, they would have a pool. Since the house we bought didn't have one, we began the process of interviewing pool contractors. We met with several. Then one day, driving down the road, we noticed a storefront for a company that installed pools. We stopped in, met the people, and then instead of taking time to research them, we signed on the dotted line. As we sat across from the salesperson, the Holy Spirit said in my spirit, very clearly, "This pool will never get finished." I brushed it off as lack of faith, but I should have known better. I knew that voice.

Not listening to that voice resulted in a nightmare. Our project dragged on and on. Two years later, our pool sat half done when the truth came out that our contractor was a crook. He was in deep debt and going under. So, to diminish his demise, he took money from large projects like ours to quickly finish smaller projects; this left the rest of us with half-done or barely started pool projects. At that point, he closed the business, and we heard he was off to jail. That pool project, by that company, was never completed. And it took us months more to find someone to come in and fix all the mistakes and finish the project: Two and a half years for one pool. I should have heeded the check in my spirit that the Holy Spirit had given me.

Can you identify gifts you had early in your life? Have you always had a tender heart of mercy? Or, maybe you were born to sing or play an instrument. God puts gifts within us all.

When I was about fifteen years old, I had a friend a couple years older than me who was struggling with being a young man and the freedoms that it afforded him. One day, he and a friend drank some beer and took his dune buggy out for a drive and crashed it. Of course, his parents found out about it and put him under some pretty severe restrictions.

At that same time, I had a baby hamster as a pet. She was not very friendly and would bite my fingers when I attempted to pick her up. By biting the hand that sought to give her freedom, she often missed out on running around on my bed or taking a stroll in her hamster ball.

One evening, I was sitting looking at my hamster in her cage as I prayed for my friend. And I heard the Lord tell me that my friend was similar to my hamster. He was living under restrictive penalty because he was "biting the hand" that sought to give him freedom. God wanted to bless him and provide for him, but he was making dangerous decisions that now resulted in penalties limiting his freedom.

I knew deep within me that I had to share this revelation with him. But it's intimidating to be a fifteen-year-old girl that has a mandate to confront a seventeen-year-old boy with a word from God. So, I first went to his parents with what God had told me, and they gave their blessing to talk to him. To my surprise, he received the word and told me how much it meant to him that a friend cared enough to pray for him and bring him a word from the Lord.

I believe the gift of counsel was birthing within me. But this gift requires humility; and it requires an ear to hear God.

Over the years, I've had many instances of clear understanding, direction, and words from God. I never thought it strange. I've just known that I speak to God and He speaks to me.

Have you ever felt that you knew something you really didn't have any way of knowing in the natural? This is what it's like to hear from God. I call it getting a "heads-up."

How you respect this gift will determine how it is portioned to you. Do you ignore it? The ability to hear will lessen. Do you listen? Your hearing will sharpen. Do you cherish it? It will increase.

I've always encouraged people to journal what they hear from God. Whether in their spirit, through dreams, in words from others: In whatever way the words come, it's important to capture them. Firstly, it says you value the importance of the words. Secondly, you'll be amazed at particular details as you look back.

Because God moves outside of time, many words that come are outside of time. By recording them, you can go back and refresh your memory on what was spoken.

Another thing God was doing in those early years was preparing me to be able to spend time alone to fulfill my calling as a leader. Leaders are often called to walk a path apart; there will not always be other leaders nearby to commune with. Often, our communion with God will sustain us. And I've walked this road most of my life.

The challenge is to not give in to self-pity, because pity is pitiful. But God will sometimes call us to walk roads that may be difficult in order to strengthen something within us. For me, though I have often been called to walk a road alone, I have not been called to walk a lonely road. The Holy Spirit is my companion.

As I shared earlier, in addition to this road presenting itself as friends who have distanced themselves, I've sometimes seen this road as distancing within my family.

My parents are two of my heroes. I try every day to be as dedicated to God as my dad is and as gracious and serving to others as my mom is. Two godly parents that serve the Lord; love others; care for their children, grandchildren, and great-grandchildren; and have been married for over sixty years. They are examples to all.

I can tell you, there is no such thing as a perfect parent; just as there are no perfect children, no perfect people. We all struggle, we all celebrate victories, we all mourn, we all make our way the best we can. But my parents are exceptional people. And I have always admired them.

Growing up, my siblings and I all had struggles at one point or another. And it was because of the struggles of some of my older siblings that my childhood changed quite a bit at the age of twelve.

When I was a young child, our family would take vacations to various places throughout the southeastern US. Camping was our go-to method of vacationing, though there were a few times we borrowed a friend's mountain cabin or rented a motel room. It was fun: swimming in pools, roasting marshmallows, tubing down rivers. I have fond memories of it all.

Family vacations ceased about the time I became a teen. My oldest sister left home when I was twelve; she had struggles no parent wants a child to experience. Not much later, my second-oldest sister moved out on her own—getting her first apartment with a friend. Fun independence, but I missed her. And then a couple years after that, my brother was gone; under unfortunate circumstances that again grieved my parents.

We didn't do too much in the way of family outings after my oldest sister left. I watched my parents go through a lot of anguish in the years that followed. This was the same time I was transitioning into the difficult middle school years. I'm so glad I had an ear to hear God in this time. This relationship has sustained me through many difficult times.

What have you done to pursue your calling?

If you feel you have a call in an area, what have you done to move toward it? Do you need a college degree to do what you feel called to do? Go get one. Do you need to know how to use a certain computer program? Learn it. Does your call require you to speak a new language? Take some classes.

On my job, part of providing equine-assisted services for individuals is getting certified as a therapeutic riding instructor. The actual instruction is not part of what I do for the organization, but I got certified so that I understand the process. That way, I support my staff with a clearer picture of their jobs. And since staff management is part of my job, this makes me a better boss.

You may not need to make big-time budgetary commitments to improve or prepare yourself. Doing research, reading a book, taking an online course, spending time volunteering: all these can help prepare you in the area to which you feel called.

Let me share an example of how God speaks, over time, to direct us.

Back in 2015, while I was working a job I did not want, I was awakened one morning at 5:12 by the vibration of something very large being dropped to earth. Later that day, as I was sitting at my computer, I suddenly heard a name dropped into my spirit: Levi.

Two days later, again: Levi.

Several months later, in January 2016, Super Bowl number fifty was played at Levi Stadium, the home of the 49ers. I realized at that time that I was a 49er (forty-nine years old), about to be fifty.

The tribe of Levi was the priestly tribe that ministered within the lands of the other eleven tribes, including within the six cities of refuge (see Joshua 20).

Fast forward to 2020. Our church was holding our annual prophetic conference just prior to Easter weekend; only, due to the coronavirus, it was a virtual conference.

Doug Addison was one of our featured speakers. He brought us an incredible message and spoke several prophetic words over our church and our city. At one point, he referred to our city of Apopka and our church, Thrive Church Apopka, as cities of refuge.

I believe that word, and the word I had received several years prior, were one in the same.

The term "city of refuge" has jumped out at me many times over the years. And each time, I wondered why. I believe God had planted a seed within me.

In Bible times, the roads leading into the Hebraic cities of refuge were clearly marked with signposts that read "Miklat," meaning "refuge." (*www.ifcj.org*)

When Chris and I decided to name our little farm in the heart of Apopka, Miklat Farm was the name we chose. Refuge Farm; dedicated to the Lord and as a place of refuge and help for the people of Apopka. Our desire is to create a haven of healing and ministry incorporating horses.

When we purchased that farm, it was a rundown, foreclosed, old house on two acres of overgrown land. Renovating our home has been one of our biggest challenges. We moved to temporary housing three times in two months before ultimately moving into and living in our house while it was under renovation. Moving room to room as the renovations progressed brought us months of drywall dust, water outages, ant infestations, and more. It was tough, but we had a goal. We knew a beautiful home and property could rise from the ashes. And we believed this property was the impetus for launching a ministry to our city.

We went after this calling like money was not an issue. That doesn't mean we spent beyond our means. We did have a budget, but we had to make great, personal sacrifices to achieve where we are at this point. And there is far to go still, and we believe God will provide a way. He'll make all things possible because we believe. And we are putting actions behind our faith.

Just weeks ago, I did a study on the history of my city. And I discovered that the Seminole tribe, which gave our city its name, came to this area as refugees fleeing Alabama and Georgia. They established this place as a city of refuge! Incredible!

We have a Levi call to a city of refuge.

Do you feel that you have natural giftings or desires in certain areas? What do you think you are good at? Perhaps you daydream about doing something or studying certain books. What topic of conversation do you find yourself drawn to? All of these are ways to self-identify clues to what you are called to do and who you are.

It's true for us all. No one else is called to do specifically what we are each individually called to do. Our work and our testimonies are important to the kingdom.

This may be as specific as you having a knack for getting spots out of fabric that nobody else can. Maybe you are good at working with numbers; or, perhaps you like doing presentations. Do people tell you that you have a good sense of style? Or, maybe they complement your makeup application. These could all point to your calling.

It was in pursing my education that one area of my calling came alive. My love for missions, and the various forms that takes, ignited once again in the summer of '99. Studying abroad for a semester turned out to be more than an educational adventure; it was my mission to Italy.

CHAPTER 3:

Mission to Italy

❧

"You're braver than you believe, stronger than you seem, and smarter than you think." Christopher Robin, from Pooh's Grand Adventure: The Search for Christopher Robin

I HAVE NEVER CONSIDERED myself a thrill-seeker. I have done some fun things as they have come to me, but I've never sought out nail-biting adventures.

As a kid, I rode roller coasters and river rapids if the group was doing these things. But for me, real joy comes from a slow horseback ride through Florida's backwoods, sitting by the winter fire with a cup of coffee and a soft blanket, laughing with friends over dinner and chatting the hours away. These things fill my tank.

I have a top-ten list of memories that are pure and utter joy. Two of these occurred the year I graduated from college.

Though I started college in my twenties, a large gap of time-off from my studies meant that I was in my thirties by the time I completed my bachelor's degree. But it was early in my studies that I took a humanities course that really opened my eyes to life beyond my little world.

The class was on the Renaissance period. We studied the art and culture of that time, and I was intrigued. I believe to this day it was the instructor's enthusiasm that captivated me. I caught her love of all things Renaissance. And if you're studying the Renaissance, you are, by default, studying Italy; therefore, I also caught the love of Italy.

My instructor made Italy and the Renaissance come alive for me. And there was one artistic piece she told of that drew me in like no other—Michelangelo's David.

The David is a seventeen-feet-tall marble statue of a young, future-king David facing his foe, Goliath. Michelangelo sculpted David over a four-year period, between 1501 and

1504. Today, the sculpture stands in the Galleria dell'Accademia in Florence, Italy.

It would be seven years after first learning about The David that I would make the trip over to see the sculpture in person.

I had just completed my bachelor's degree, and the owner of the company I was interning with had offered me a full-time position. But before committing to a lifetime of full-time work, he wondered if I wanted to take some time off that summer. "Why yes," I had been waiting years to say. "I plan to study abroad for the summer. I'm going to Italy."

It was a big decision. I was a newly single adult in my thirties, transitioning from part-time to full-time work, with college loans to pay off. Could I afford to spend a summer in Europe? It was calling to me. But was it wise?

I spent the months leading up to that summer praying, counseling with friends, and taking long runs talking to God. Was I crazy to think I could do this?

Six months before the trip, the deposit was due. It was just $200.00, but it may as well have been $20,000.00. I did not have it, so I went to God in prayer.

"Lord, You know I feel like I'm supposed to go to Italy to study this summer. I've wanted to go for years. But the deposit is due tomorrow. If I'm supposed to go, I need $200.00."

I went home, opened my mailbox, and there was a check for $200.00. Unknown to me, several months back, I had miscalculated the payoff of my car and overpaid by $200.00. The refund came the day it was needed.

And just like that, I was all in on my mission to Italy.

Our traveling university group joined students from another American university to study at the University of Urbino, in Urbino, Italy. We lived in the dorms located in the mountainous hills surrounding the historic city. It was an unbelievable trip.

The City of Urbino is the birthplace of one of the four most well-known artists of Renaissance, and Ninja Turtle fame, Raphael. And the fifteenth-century city does not disappoint—from cobblestone streets to the turrets of Ducale Palace high above. It is like a step back in time.

The walled-in city features incredibly steep roads that challenged the calf muscles of the American students in our group. Thankfully, I was a runner in those days and handled the morning walks down from our dorms in the mountains and up into the city center with no trouble. But there was an elevator at the city gate for those who couldn't muster the walk up.

Shops, restaurants, businesses, and residences line the streets of the city, with the majestic Ducale Palace in city center, across from the university. A large stone fountain sits in the middle of the piazza and is a gathering spot each evening for wine, laughter, and lingering.

Italian life is quite different than what I was used to. The quaint, little mountain village of Urbino woke up slowly. Breakfast was coffee and pastry.

The group I was traveling with from my university back home was a split group. About half of the students were in their twenties and the other half were older, retired men and women. A lovely benefit of the university program allows senior citizens to study for free. They pay for their travel expenses and get the opportunity to learn in the university and on field trips alongside all the younger students. And it was a wonderful experience to be the only thirty-something in the midst of our group of young college kids and much older but energetic senior students.

One Saturday morning, I was walking through the Urbino farmer's market and came upon some of the older members of our group. They recognized me and stopped to ask if I had come across any places where they could get bacon and eggs. Sorry, no; we were far from our American norms.

On days we had classes, the American students would gather in the city square to say good morning and enjoy a slow start to the day. Most of the 13,000-plus regular university students were away for the summer, which left just the town residents and a few hundred American students that July and August. It was like we had our own town.

After breakfast greetings, we were off to classes. The rest of the day consisted of class lectures, lunch in the university cafeteria, afternoon siesta, study time, dinner at the cafeteria or in town with friends, more studying, and then bedtime. And by the way, cafeteria food in an Italian university is no joke. I'm talking four-course meals every night, featuring entrees of everything from gnocchi to arancini di riso (rice balls). So good!

I had two college courses at the Universita` di Urbino—Italian Culture and Renaissance Art History.

My Italian culture instructor was a native Italian man who had traveled over with us from our American university to teach classes in Italy. I knew him well; I had taken my Italian language classes under his tutelage.

The instructor for my art class was an American woman who had lived in Italy for many years. And her love and passion for Renaissance art matched that of the instructor who had sparked my interest so many years prior.

However, it was the weekly field trips that were the highlight of our studies. We actually went to see the art that we were studying. Some of the highlights were Rome, where I visited the Sistine Chapel and had an audience with the pope; Assisi, where I bought paintings from local artisans; Florence, where I saw The David and journaled in the piazza; Venice, well, what's not to love about Venice; Fano, where I lay on the beach with an artist friend while she sketched and did watercolors; and Macerata, where we attended an open-air opera of Shakespeare's *Othello*. But one of my top-ten moments actually came right there in the heart of Urbino, in the university's college of music.

It was a Monday evening in mid-July. The weather was cooler than usual that night. Because we were in a mountainous region, the summer was typically pleasantly warm in the day and comfortably cool in the evening.

That night, the instructors from the school of music had planned an outdoor performance in city center. But due to the extra nip in the air, the concert was moved inside. I just love a culture that can up and move an entire event and the townspeople don't complain. They just walked down the street and up three flights of stairs to the top floor of one of the university's music rooms.

The room was not large, but we all comfortably squeezed in. I managed a seat that gave me a view of the performers and the open, floor-to-ceiling windows behind them. Out the nighttime window, the lights from a town on a distant mountain twinkled. The pianist lulled us with his magical melodies and, one by one, the performers serenaded us in song.

The pinnacle of the concert, to me, was the soprano. She took us high and low with her operatic performance. And as she sang, I looked beyond her into the night, with the cool breeze blowing in off the mountains. The twinkling, distant lights causing my mind to drift, drift. My body grounded in that room, in a wooden chair, on a wooden floor. But my soul drifting out the open windows, floating into the cool night sky, high above the mountain peaks as the music called me outward and upward. As I listened, this thought came to me—*I'll never experience this moment again, and I'll never forget it.* And I never have. That room, that music, that night are forever etched in my mind as a magical night of remembrance.

It was just weeks later and miles away when I experienced one of my other top-ten memories.

Summer 1999, University of Urbino, Italy

The David

In early August, one of our "field trips" was a double-stop adventure to Rome and Florence. This visit to Florence was what had brought me on this trip.

The day had finally arrived: I was to see Michelangelo's David.

It's all very dramatic to visit The David. You enter the galleria and walk the halls, looking at the various art pieces. When suddenly, you turn a corner and there in front of you, at the end of the hall, is the glorious statue elevated up on its pedestal.

He stands within a domed room with white-paneled walls; a space dedicated to him alone. He can be viewed in 360 degrees. And as I walked around him, my head bent back looking up, I saw in amazement what my humanities instructor had described so many years before.

Remarkably, you see a different David, depending on the angle from which you view him.

From the front, you see a confident young man in his prime. His stance is one of self-assuredness, with his weight cocked back on one leg as he looks to his left. His hand, holding the famous sling and stone, rests up on his shoulder. It is the moment just before he rears back to lose the fateful blow that defeats his enemy, Goliath.

And then I walked to the right and stood face to face with David; his gaze, over my head and beyond me, to Goliath, his towering, giant foe. And David is no longer a self-assured warrior. His look is now one of terror. His piercing stare says, "This enemy is giant! I'm just a teenage boy! What have I gotten myself into?" What had, at other angles, appeared as a cocky, young man in his prime now looked like a scared boy coiled back in fear.

The change in confidence, brought about merely by my vantage point, taught me a great lesson.

So often, we take a stance of self-assuredness to those around us. We may even fool ourselves. And then we look at our foes. We realize that we wrestle not with flesh and blood, but our enemy is formidable, much as David's Goliath was. We're in for a fight much larger than ourselves. It's only when we look from God's vantage point that we see we are undefeatable; not because of who we are, but because of who God is.

> *We're in for a fight much larger than ourselves. It's only when we look from God's vantage point that we see we are undefeatable; not because of who we are, but because of who God is.*

David knew that the battle was not his alone. His God was much bigger than his enemy.

David said to the Philistine, "You come against me with sword and spear and javelin, but I come against you in the name of the Lord Almighty, the God of the armies of Israel, whom you have defied. This day the Lord will deliver you into my hands, and I'll strike you down and cut off your head. This very day I will give the carcasses of the Philistine army to the birds and the wild animals, and the whole world will know that there is a God in Israel. All those gathered here will know that it is not by sword or spear that the Lord saves; for the battle is the Lord's, and He will give all of you into our hands." 1 Samuel 17: 45-47 (NIV)

Many times in my life, I've had to stand on this Scripture. Even as I've been writing this book, in the middle of the worldwide pandemic of coronavirus, I've put these verses into practice.

We've walked through some very difficult, personal times within our family this past year; things no family ever wants to go through. And on one of the darkest days, I looked out on our pool deck in time to see a deadly, venomous coral snake. I immediately grabbed a shovel, went to him, and cut off his head. And as I did so, I proclaimed loudly to the enemy, "You'll not have our family, enemy! I cut off your head!"

The battle is not mine alone. I gird myself with the tools God has provided and go to the battle, but He gives me the victory.

That day in Florence, Italy, was seven years in the waiting, but it was also a lesson that was a lifetime in the making. God was birthing something new in me. And the fruits of that trip were just beginning to show.

Summer 1999, Seeing The David

Dorm Life

Living in a dorm was a new experience for me.

I didn't go away to college. I always lived at home or had an apartment nearby with a roommate.

But that summer in Italy, I experienced what it was like to live among strangers and share bathrooms and a kitchen with a group of younger girls.

When you grow up in church and hang out with friends from church, sometimes you miss out on the opportunity to spend time with the unchurched. But that summer, I got to meet all kinds of people.

Within the group was a girl that smoked and cussed like a sailor. She was full of anger and difficult to be around. Most people preferred not to, but I decided I would be her friend.

By the end of that European summer, I learned she had conquered cancer three times in her young life. And while we were on that trip, she got the call that her latest test results showed the cancer was back.

I don't consider my life any more important or any more perfect than anyone else. I think I'm finding my way the same as everyone else. The choices I make often come at great, personal sacrifice because I believe in a greater purpose. And, sometimes, the choices I make set me up for success and personal satisfaction. Either way, I'm grateful for the lessons, the growth, and the rewards. That summer in Italy, my choices did not go unnoticed.

I lived my life no differently in those Italian dorm rooms than I did back home in Florida. I spent time alone with God. I read my Bible. And I made decisions for abstinence and sobriety. One day, sitting in the kitchen reading my Bible, one of the girls from our dorm walked in. "That looks like a Bible," she said. That led to a discussion; and more people joined in. I was able to share my testimony. I told about my divorce, the loss of my baby, and how God had been with me and healed me from those losses.

Over the course of the summer, I was amazed at the questions those girls asked, like what's it like dealing with people when I minister the gospel (referring to my time doing jail ministry in my early twenties), to which I shared about the justice of God. Questions about whether I thought Jesus was really the Son of God or just a great prophet, to which I shared the loving mercy of God. Questions on whether I hoped for a romantic opportunity with a guy while in Italy, to which I shared the humility of walking with God. The opportunities to share my faith were endless.

From my Italian journal:

The trip has been a great witness opportunity. I thought this trip would be a time for me to get away with God, just Him and me. I thought I'd get great insight into myself through time alone with Him. Instead, I've learned about myself by giving of myself to others. I've learned to witness. I've learned to be genuine. I haven't been perfect. I've been in bad moods, I've complained, I've not felt well. But I've grown by being here. Being immersed in the world has strengthened my resolve.

I don't know if I'll get to lead anyone to Christ. I don't yet know if I'll get to pray with anyone. But I know my life has made a difference. And I know I may be the only one praying that [name retracted] will be healed of lymphatic cancer and that [name retracted]'s liver will be accepted by her body instead of rejected, and so on. If I only came here to have a positive influence on these girls, it was worth it.

I was so concerned about the cost of this trip before I came. But now that I'm here, I realize that there is no price too great to pay to help a soul move toward God.

*These girls are all so precious. I hope that I can
continue to present my life as a godly example
in humility.*

I don't know what living my life for God did personally for
any of the people around me. But I do know that the young
lady in her fourth round of cancer stayed in touch with me
for a couple years after that summer. And I was able to be a
listening ear and caring heart for her two years later when
her new husband was killed in a car accident.

Oh, Venice

There were so many wonderful memories made during my
summer semester in Italy. I traveled to places and saw things
I never thought I would. One of my favorite fun memories
is from our final week in the country. We were on our field
trip to Venice. Oh, Venice. How I love you.

It's such a romantic city. I actually would not allow myself
to ride in a gondola. Because it was so romantic, I just
could not do it by myself. I decided I'd return some day
to ride with my future husband. (He still owes me a trip,
by the way.)

While in Venice, I went out walking the city one night with a
gal from the other university that was part of our group. We
had dinner at a lovely restaurant and continued to explore

the back alleys and little shops for hours. When suddenly, we heard Frank Sinatra music coming from somewhere.

Upon investigation, we stumbled upon an open-air bar decorated with "I ♥ NY," New York Yankees memorabilia, Statue of Liberty décor, and all other kinds of New York paraphernalia. But the thing that really caught our attention was that the bar was full of American GIs.

As soon as they caught sight of us, the bartender shouted out, "Who do we have in the house?!" To which my northern friend replied, "Connecticut!" This caused the bartender to respond, "We got Connecticut in the house!" The GIs whooped and hollered. It was great fun.

We only stayed for about an hour, but we had a good time talking with the servicemen about their families back home, where they were stationed, and their military jobs.

One group of three young men with the air force were a source of entertainment and conversation. When my friend asked one of them if he had been flying lately, his response of, "We don't all fly, ma'am;" got a good laugh. As an English major, I was regularly presented with the question, "What are you going to do with your degree, teach?" Taking a que from the young serviceman, my new response became, "We don't all teach, ma'am."

I'll always hold the summer of '99 in my memory as the summer of a lifetime. Maybe I was living my missionary dream after all.

CHAPTER 4:

Mission to Russia

"I will say to the north, 'Give them up!' and to the south, 'Do not hold them back.' Bring my sons from afar and my daughters from the ends of the earth." Isaiah 43:6 (NIV)

G OD DID ULTIMATELY restore to me all that was lost—marriage, family, home. I've been married for twenty years now to my husband, Chris. I got a bonus daughter in that deal—Nicole, who is now grown and married herself. And my lifelong desire and mandate from the Lord to adopt children came true when we brought our daughter Lexie home from Russia seventeen years ago, followed by our son, Shane, three years after that. We are blessed.

Mandate from the Lord to adopt? Yes, I believe one of the calls on my life since the time I was young was to adopt.

God has used dreams to speak to me for many years. Early on, I did not realize it was God speaking; I just thought it was part of my internal desires, which was sometimes true. I dreamt often of adopted children. They were all colors, ages, appearances, and they came to me in various ways. But the one thing that was true in each dream was that they were mine and I did not birth them.

By the time I was a young teen, I knew that someday I would adopt a child. And I also believed that child would come from another nation.

When I married Chris, he knew of and supported my desire to adopt. So, it was no surprise that three years later, we were on our way to Russia to meet our new baby girl.

Lexie was the baby of my dreams. The first time we met, she was five months old. She smiled the entire time. And so did we. Two months later, we made the long trip home with her and began raising our daughter. It was a time of unbelievably happy memories.

June 2004, in Russia with Baby Lexie

About eighteen months later, we made a plan to expand our family further by adopting again. This time, we thought we'd look locally for a child. And the more we looked, the more we realized that sibling groups and older children were so in need of families. So, we took on a sibling group of sisters: twelve, fourteen, and fifteen years old. We had no idea what we were doing. We just wanted to give those girls the blessed lives we had always had.

Parenting is difficult in the best of situations. But when you pair up teenagers who, through lack of stability, have learned to work the system, with two naive foster parents, you might just have a recipe for disaster.

Our intent was to adopt. We loved those girls. And our family of seven made many precious memories. Two of the girls accepted Jesus as their savior during their time with us. The eldest girl got to go to prom. A friend got all of us into Disney—their first visit. We bought some horses, and I enjoyed taking the girls on trail rides. We celebrated birthdays and holidays with family. We laughed around the dinner table. We poured our lives into loving those precious girls.

But ultimately, we could not keep them safe from their own risky behavior. In their brokenness from years of abuse and neglect, they could not find a way to comply with the rules that would keep them, or our two-year-old and nine-year-old, safe. The risk was too great. And for the oldest two, their desire to live their own lives resulted in their desire to not be adopted. We could not move forward with adoption. We were devastated.

Reaching the decision to not adopt our three foster daughters was a spiritual war. We counseled, we prayed, we travailed before ultimately making the heart-wrenching decision to not move forward. It was months of seeking a breakthrough, a plan, a way forward. But every indicator and counsel pointed to one end. We were not to be their adoptive parents; it wasn't what we had anticipated. Sometimes, God takes us ways we don't foresee, but we must trust Him.

Months after, Chris and I looked at each other and asked the question, "Are we done?" Had the difficulties of the past season shown us that we just didn't have what it takes to parent any additional children? We agreed that we would not be defeated. We felt we had done our best in what we had invested into the lives of those girls.

The following year, we were back in Russia, meeting the eighteen-month-old toddler who would be our son.

In the nine months of paperwork and preparation to adopt Shane, we encountered some obstacles we never anticipated. We faced a new spiritual war. And one of us nearly did not make it out alive.

The Fall

Several years earlier, on a sunny Saturday afternoon, Chris was working in the yard and I was inside tending to our daughters, Nicole and Lexie. Our two girls were about eight and one at that time. Our front yard had several large oak trees, and Chris wanted to trim some lower branches that hung twenty or so feet overhead. He prepared the ladder and chainsaw, as I instructed him to wait for me to return before beginning the job. I just needed to run inside and make lunch for the girls.

As I handed the girls their lunch, I heard the chainsaw fire up outside. He had not waited for me.

By the time I reached the front yard, I saw a large, partially cut-through limb swing down toward Chris, perched high on the ladder with the pole saw in hand. He saw the limb coming toward him and threw the saw forward, as he launched himself backward off the ladder to avoid being knocked off by the limb. He hit the ground with a thud, flat on his back. The wind knocked out of his lungs, but no real, apparent injury beyond that as he lay motionless on the ground.

I ran to him, yelling, "I told you to wait for me!" (I'm not always sympathetic in times of crisis.)

He rallied, and we thought he had dodged a bullet.

We soon found out that the fall had severely aggravated an abdominal hernia from years prior. Emergency exploratory surgery following a burst appendix when he was a teen had resulted in a large abdominal scar and weakened abdominal muscle. We had dealt with this same hernia when we were dating, but this time, the fall set off what would be five more surgeries and multiple attempts to secure his abdominal wall.

After the ladder fall, the mesh placed during the hernia repair surgery seemed to suffice. But two years later, in the midst of adoption paperwork for Shane, the problems with the previous repair began to surface, and mesh replacement surgery was necessary.

Chris was in the hospital recovering from the surgery. His family had come up from south Florida to visit him. We had just gotten home from the hospital visit, I was feeding the horses, and his family was packing up to drive back home when the phone rang.

"Mrs. Pharo. This is the hospital. You need to come back. Your husband has taken a turn for the worse."

We all piled back in the cars and rushed back. Septic shock: Chris had crashed just after we had left from our previous visit.

We were just months away from getting on a plane to go meet our son in Russia, and the doctors were telling me that my husband was in surgery for the second time that week. They believed his colon had been nicked in the previous hernia repair surgery, resulting in the sepsis. It was a long night, but the worst was yet to come.

The emergency surgery could not be completed. He was too unstable. A third surgery that week resulted in a gaping hole about the size of a dessert plate in his abdominal wall. The muscle was too traumatized, weak, and unstable to come back together. I was told that if he lived, it would close on its own, over time.

He remained unconscious, on life support, for a month; pumped full of fluids that added ninety pounds of weight in a matter of days. When I looked into his hospital room, it didn't look like my husband, but this large, lifeless, pale man with tubes and wires everywhere. A wound vac covered the hole in his stomach, which was stuffed with saline-soaked gauze; a treatment routine that I would learn to oversee at home for months to come.

He lived, though I could tell from the doctors' faces and their careful word choices they were skeptical he would.

One additional surgery before he came home; weeks of home health care nurses; and then, as I had declared we would to the doctors in the hospital hallways, we boarded a plane to Russia to meet our son. Hole in Chris's abdomen and all, we would not be stopped. We thought we had overcome our final challenge. We were wrong.

The Judge

When you have a dream, and you have a course of action that you believe in with all of your being, nothing will stop you. And when you are a mom-to-be, nothing will keep you from your child.

> *When you have a dream, and you have a course of action that you believe in with all of your being, nothing will stop you.*

Years before, when we adopted Lexie, the process was magical. The orphanage was hospitable, the court process was a breeze, and we brought home our beautiful, baby girl to family waving welcome signs at the airport.

In the months leading up to adopting Shane, our eighteen-month-old adorable boy, something sinister happened that made the national news. An American adoptive mother of a Russian boy had placed her son on a plane and returned him, alone, to Russia. She had given up. He was a troubled boy; she was overwhelmed. And instead of getting help, she packed him up and sent him on a plane across the ocean by himself.

News of this atrocity did not go unnoticed by the Russian supreme court. And they took action that affected all other adoptions currently in process and those thereafter.

Foreign adoption is not inexpensive. And Chris and I are not wealthy. Our decision to adopt internationally, twice, was life-altering. And the cost to do so was personal. Each adoption required two trips over. Airfare was costly, hotels expensive, and food in-country was pricey. The result was that we often did not eat but once or twice a day. We filled our suitcases with snacks and made do.

On each trip, we were in-country about a week to ten days. On the first trip, you meet your baby and petition the court for adoption. On the second trip, the adoption is finalized and you pick up your child. This means going before a judge to get a ruling in your favor for the adoption, and then you have to stay a few days after to finish paperwork in Moscow. The only saving grace was that there was a ten-day waiting period that followed the adoption, which the judge could choose to waive. When we adopted Lexie, the judge waived it, and we returned home just days after the adoption was finalized. We hoped for the same grace with Shane, because that extra ten days would have threatened to push us over our ability to financially support our little family.

When the news hit about the little Russian boy that was sent home, the Russian supreme court ruled that the ten-day waiting period would be mandatory for everyone from that point forward. No exceptions.

We were in shock. And we were unsure what to do. So, we prayed. And our family, friends, and church prayed for us. And we headed to Russia on our second trip, to get our son.

The day of our court appearance to hear the judge's ruling on our adoption case had come. It may seem strange to the way we are used to doing things in the US, but when you adopt internationally in Russia, there is a civil court hearing with a prosecutor, defender, and all the other roles that accompany a court case.

We were sitting in the hallway outside the courtroom, waiting for our time to appear before the judge, when our interpreter came over to speak with us. She told us that the judge was angry with us. What? Angry? We'd never met the woman.

As part of our adoption paperwork, we were required to prepare a dossier. There are hundreds of pieces of paper that go into the whole process. But one thing is a write-up that we do as a family wanting to adopt. In it, we describe our family, our home, our lives. And in our write-up, we mentioned our involvement in our church.

Chris and I were both raised in church and have continued that practice with our children. We are active members that believe in being a part of the body of Christ. And in our dossier, we described ourselves as "very" active in our church.

That description, that use of the word "very," irritated the judge. Apparently, she had recently become very involved herself in the Russian Orthodox Church. That, combined with Internet searches that uncovered cultic religious organizations in the western world, raised a flag in her mind. Somehow, she concluded that we, as a couple that was "very" active in our western church, a couple that did not share her choice of religious practice, must be involved in a cult.

When we appeared before the judge, it was obvious our interpreter had not misinterpreted the situation. The judge was angry at us.

For two and a half hours, she grilled us. The court workers were in disbelief at her demeanor and actions. She questioned our choice of church, friends, beliefs, and financial giving to the church. We were being persecuted for our religious beliefs.

The judge only allowed my normally quiet, reserved husband to speak. Only once did she address me, asking just one question. I'm of the belief that my very direct, authoritative response took me out of the running as our representative. She had me sit and continued on with her line of questioning to Chris.

Her question to me was an inquiry on why most of our friend group is part of our church. My response, intently staring into her eyes, was, "Because that's what we choose. We could choose friends from anywhere. But these are good people. We like them. It's our choice to be friends with them."

At the end of it all, she grilled us, she lectured us, she did not like us, but she did grant us our son. And that was that.

The only obstacle to overcome was the now-mandatory ten-day waiting period. We had anticipated an additional four to five days of paperwork, but we were still praying for a release to return home at the end of those few days. The supreme court of Russia was not on our side. The angry Russian judge was not on our side. But the God of heaven was on our side. We don't know to this day what happened, but we received notice that we did not have to stay the additional ten days. We could take our son home.

Chris survived the trip; his abdomen eventually did grow back together. And our two babies are now both high schoolers.

2008, Meeting Baby Shane in Russia

CHAPTER 5:

All the King's Horses

❦

"The horse is made ready for the day of battle, but the victory belongs to the Lord." Proverbs 21:31 (EST)

I HAVE LOVED HORSES my whole life. I was the kid in the family car that yelled out, "Horse!" every time we passed a roadside field. I drove my siblings crazy reading the horse classified ads aloud from the Sunday newspaper every week. I wanted everyone to know all the awesome horses that were available to own!

Growing up, my family was your average middle-class family in the 1980s. My dad worked an office job; my mom alternated between stay-at-home mom and working in the kitchen of the school near our house, so that we would not get bused across town. Though by the time I was in fourth grade, Mom must have taken an office job, because my final three years of elementary school were miles from home in south Orlando.

I didn't realize at the time that my being bused to a school far from home was part of the government's plan to help end segregation, but I'm glad I was a part of it. I liked my school, and I liked my friends—of all shapes, sizes, and colors.

My family had two cars and one TV—with three channels. We ate dinner around the table together, we read books, we played games, and we went to church.

And one "magical" day, on my sixteenth birthday, I received an incredible gift: my first horse.

I realize now what an absolute blessing it was to be given a horse. We were not an equestrian-level family (i.e., we were not wealthy). But God was merciful. We got a good deal. And my horse Rooster was healthy and relatively inexpensive to own. Rooster was my life.

Me at sixteen, with my first horse, Rooster

He lived at a small boarding barn three miles from my house, where I'd go daily to groom, ride, bathe, and graze him. I spent long summer days with him, taking afternoon naps in the hay barn and catching rides to horse shows and tack auctions from some of the adult ladies that boarded horses at the same barn.

Years later, Chris and I bought horses for our family, and my kids had the opportunity to experience horse ownership.

None of them share my love for horses, but I'm grateful I got to live the horse life with them while they were young.

My love for horses has never waned. Today, I work for a nonprofit that provides opportunity for individuals with special needs and those with trauma to experience the healing and restorative gifts that God put within equine. I'm regularly amazed at how special horses are. Pardon me for a minute while I share some of my favorite horse facts about why they are so effective in helping those with physical, mental, and emotional needs.

Interestingly, a horse's walking gait closely resembles a human's. And riding them causes an individual's core to engage in the same manner—forward and back, up and down, and rotationally. For those with limited or no mobility, riding a horse not only strengthens muscles; it is highly satisfactory because it feels like walking.

Another thing that happens is that the motion and movement of a horse's rocking, swaying walk engages the muscles that are used in speech. For this reason, it's not uncommon for individuals that previously have never spoken to utter their first words from horseback.

Horses are prey animals; meaning, in nature, they are food to other animals. This constant threat to their safety causes them to always be on alert. A horse's number-one priority is to not get eaten. In the primary choices for safety—fight or flight—they choose flight if at all possible.

This need to get away from predators causes horses to be hyper-aware. They are always looking, always listening, and almost always on their feet. Horses primarily sleep standing up and only lie down for twenty to thirty minutes in a twenty-four-hour period.

They mistrust anything or anyone they do not know. The enemy could be a wolf, a person, or a plastic bag blowing in the wind. They are never willing to take a chance on anything that looks, sounds, or smells scary. If you want to be near a horse and interact with it, you must earn its trust.

One incredible benefit of being around horses is that a horse's resting heart rate is much lower than a human's. And by just being near a horse, your heart rate will slow down to match the horse's heart rate. This brings a sense of calm.

All of these characteristics make them excellent partners in the healing process for those with PTSD, anxiety, depression, anger issues, and such. They demand self-regulation; they demand trust be earned; they mirror what fear and triggers look like. It's amazing how helpful this is in the healing process for many.

But even though horses are super cool, and beautiful, and useful, they cannot meet all our needs. They can't save us, or heal us, or restore us. They are helpful in the efforts, but something more is needed.

The well-known nursery rhyme "Humpty Dumpty" tells of an anthropomorphized egg that takes a tumble off a high place and cannot be restored by human efforts.

> *Humpty Dumpty sat on a wall,*
> *Humpty Dumpty had a great fall.*
> *All the king's horses and all the king's men*
> *Couldn't put Humpty together again.*
> (Arnold)

Though it may not have been the author's original intent, this message is common to all of mankind. At some point, we all fall from our perch and find ourselves in need of rescue and repair.

Horses are not healers, but God created them to help in the process. Only the King can fix the broken. Only the King of Kings can set mankind right and put our lives back together. Not the King's horses; not His men; just the King.

At some point, we will be knocked from our perches and need justice. We will knock others from their perches and need mercy. We will have fallen from our perches and need humility. We'll need the King.

I have needed all three; sometimes, all at the same time.

At some point, we will be knocked from our perches and need justice. We will knock others from their perches and need mercy. We will have fallen from our perches and need humility. We'll need the King.

CHAPTER 6

Do the Love Walk

❦

"He has told you, O man, what is good; and what does the Lord require of you but to do justice, and to love kindness, and to walk humbly with your God?" Micah 6:8 (ESV)

M Y PERSONAL JOURNEY of stepping into what God has called me to do has involved some physical and spiritual groundwork. Learning what true love looks like and how to truly live a life of humility has been a big part of my process. And being open to the various ways in which God teaches and instructs has been a learning process in its own right.

Last night, I had three dreams. Since I have not remembered many dreams as of late, three in one night had me journaling and seeking interpretation.

The first dream was about recreating a scene between a slave man and a free man in order to show the injustice that was done.

The second dream was about rescuing two baby snow owls that were taken from their nest.

The third was about a horse that was hooked up to a buckboard full of people and made to walk backward, awkwardly pushing it behind him rather than pulling it forward.

Praying about the interpretation, the Holy Spirit showed me that the dreams pointed to Micah 6:8.

The first dream was a call to justice for the man who was wronged. The second dream has a deeper personal meaning, but caring for the orphaned baby owls was a call to love mercy. And the third dream about the horse forced to walk backward was a demonstration of walking humbly.

I receive these dreams as confirmation that I'm on the right track in writing *this* book. I knew I was supposed to write *a* book. I've had several confirmations on that. And each time, I would tell the Lord that I didn't *need* to write a book. What would it be about?

I've never had a message I felt I was to deliver, or a system of doing something I needed to share. But I do believe our lives, our testimonies, hold power for others in the sharing. In Revelation 12:11 (NKJV), John tells us that *"they overcame him by the blood of the Lamb and by the word of their testimony."* We see this in the setting of a heavenly courtroom. Verse 10 tells us that Satan, the accuser of our brethren, stands before God day and night, accusing us all. But that the accuser has been cast down. And the legal verdict of victory is ours because of the blood of the Lamb, and because we sat in that witness box and testified.

What is that testimony? It's speaking up about how Jesus has come to our rescue, about how He has been present in our lives. It's sharing what He has done. There is power in that. We win the court case because of Jesus and because we open our mouths and testify. This book is my testimony. It's powerful. Not because I'm writing it, but because He said I would overcome my accuser by sharing it; this book is obedience.

And what is Micah 6:8 about? It's about obedience. What does the Lord require of you? Is it sacrifice? No, it's obedience. Do justice, love mercy, walk humbly.

First Samuel 15:22 tells us that to obey is better than sacrifice. Yes, He will forgive us and cover us. But obedience would be better than going down the road of disobedience, consequence, forgiveness, and restoration.

I love how Micah 6:8 paints a picture of God's courtroom.

Justice is a legal term. God is the ultimate judge. Psalm 75:7 (NKJV) says, "*God is the Judge.*" Isaiah 33:22 (KJV) says, "*The Lord is our judge, the Lord is our lawgiver, the Lord is our king.*" James 4:12 (NIV) tells us, "*There is only one Lawgiver and Judge, the One who is able to save and to destroy.*" These are just a few samples of the many scriptures that speak of God as judge. And He is a just God that demands justice.

Micah goes on to speak about loving mercy. What does any defendant want from the judge? They want mercy. And God requires that we love mercy. We are to demonstrate the same type of ruling that has been given to us. He was merciful, and we should show mercy.

And what about the walk of humility? Can't you just picture a person of guilt being granted a ruling of mercy. Their walk would be one of humbleness. They were pardoned of their guilt; they bear no sentence for their sin. If we have been saved by the grace of God, that should change how we view ourselves. We should walk in victory, yes. But we should walk in recognition of the great price that was paid on our behalf. Jesus took our sentencing. He took our guilty verdict. He paid the penalty. It was His death. We walk free. That makes me want to walk in humble gratitude. What about you?

Another Scripture very similar to Micah 6 is Isaiah 58 (KJV). Verse 2 says that God's people keep coming to Him, trying to impress Him with their fasting and asking for "*ordinances of justice.*"

> "'*Why have we fasted,' they say, 'and you have not seen it? Why have we humbled ourselves, and you have not noticed?'*" (Isa. 58:3, NIV)

Sound familiar? Isn't our sacrifice enough? We fasted, aren't you pleased?

But God says they need to be made aware of their sin and rebellion. Their fast is a pious one.

And His response is familiar too.

> Verse 6 (NKJV)—Justice. "*Is this not the fast that I have chosen: To loose the bonds of wickedness, to undo the heavy burdens, to let the oppressed go free, and that you break every yoke?*"

Verse 7 (NKJV)—Mercy. "*Is it not to share your bread with the hungry, and that you bring to your house the poor who are cast out; when you see the naked, that you cover him, and not hide yourself from your own flesh?*"

Verse 8-10 (NKJV)—Humility. "*Then your light shall break forth like the morning, your healing shall spring forth speedily, and your righteousness shall go before you; the glory of the Lord shall be your rear guard. Then you shall call, and the Lord will answer; you shall cry, and He will say, 'Here I am.' If you take away the yoke from your midst, the pointing of the finger, and speaking wickedness, if you extend your soul to the hungry and satisfy the afflicted soul, then your light shall dawn in the darkness, and your darkness shall be as the noonday.*"

Yes, fasting is good and it's required, but it's not a show of holiness on the faster's part. God wants us instead to love, serve, and care for others.

This justice, mercy, and humility thing isn't a one-time thing. It's a lifestyle; it's a walk.

Do Justice

> *"Evil men do not understand justice, but*
> *those who seek the Lord understand all."*
> *Proverbs 28:5 (NKJV)*

I've heard Philippians 4:7 most of my life, but I never stopped to really listen to those words until recently. The part that caught my attention is *"the peace of God, which surpasses understanding."*

There is a peace that we have access to that by our situation, by our circumstances, should not be. When human reasoning says everything is a mess, stress is high, there is no hope, God says He gives us peace. Even though it doesn't make sense, there is peace in the midst of it all. The reality of this peace surpasses our human understanding. How can it be? The answer is in verse 6.

> *"Be anxious for nothing, but in everything by*
> *prayer and supplication, with thanksgiving, let*
> *your requests be made known to God; and the*
> *peace of God, which surpasses all understanding,*
> *will guard your hearts and minds through Christ*
> *Jesus."* (Phil. 4:6-7, NKJV)

There it is. We do our part first. In Greek, the statement "*be anxious for nothing*" is actually saying behave carefully, take thought, be careful.

So, we are instructed to carefully and thoughtfully pray in thankfulness, asking for what we need. Then God does His part. He gives unexplainable peace, and He guards our hearts and minds. So many times in my life, I've lived this out.

Recently, a member of my family has been in a difficult place. By all earthly standards, I should be a wreck. But I'm not.

I love that family member so much. I hurt deeply for the hurt that person feels. There are moments when I have to war through for my peace of mind and my family member's victory. But I'm sleeping at night. I'm eating pretty well. I'm able to form coherent sentences on paper. I have a peace that surpasses my understanding.

Paul goes on to provide additional instruction, because attacks against the mind take persistent warfare.

> "*Finally, brethren, whatever things are true, whatever things are noble, whatever things are just, whatever things are pure, whatever things are lovely, whatever things are of good report, if there is any virtue and if there is anything praiseworthy—meditate on these things. The*

things which you learned and received and heard
and saw in me, these do, and the God of peace
will be with you." (Phil. 4:8-9, NKJV)

It's right there! This is how we battle the assault against our minds. We choose what we think on: things that are true, noble (honest), just, pure, lovely, of good report (reputable), virtuous, praiseworthy.

When worry tries to throw what-ifs at me, I knock them down with my buckler (see Psalm 91:4 about this awesome weapon that is both defensive and offensive in war). And I choose to remember fun times, or a sweet moment, or a blessing that I received. Often, I force myself to sing praise songs, or make up songs from Scripture or declarations over myself, my family, my home, my city. This is the sacrifice of praise. It's powerful. It changes the atmosphere.

Here are some other Scriptures that you can declare to over-come mental attacks or assaults on your peace. Read them out loud, turn them into songs, memorize them, etc.

"You will keep him in perfect peace, whose mind
is stayed on You, because he trusts in You." Isaiah
26:3 (NKJV)

"Jesus said to him, 'You shall love the Lord your
God with all your heart, with all your soul, and

with all your mind.' This is the first and great commandment." Matthew 22:37-38 (NKJV)

"We demolish arguments and every pretension that sets itself up against the knowledge of God, and we take captive every thought to make it obedient to Christ." 2 Corinthians 10:5 (NIV)

"When you lie down, you shall not be afraid; yes, you will lie down and your sleep will be sweet." Proverbs 3:24 (AMPC)

"Be anxious for nothing, but in everything by prayer and supplication, with thanksgiving, let your requests be made known to God; and the peace of God, which surpasses all understanding, will guard your hearts and minds through Christ Jesus." Philippians 4:6-7 (NKJV)

"For God has not given us a spirit of fear, but of power and of love and of a sound mind." 2 Timothy 1:7 (KJV)

"In the multitude of my anxieties within me, your comforts delight my soul." Psalm 94:19 (NKJV)

"I will both lie down in peace, and sleep; for You alone, O Lord, make me dwell in safety." Psalm 4:8 (NKJV)

My socially-conscious teenage daughter, Lexie, and I are on a walk, and she asks if I understand the difference between equality and justice.

This is how many of our conversations begin. She becomes aware of a social issue. She researches it online, she watches videos about it, she investigates how pertinent political figures feel on the issue, she discusses it with friends, and then she brings it into our conversations. She is an activist. She is concerned for the marginalized, the down-trodden, and anyone who doesn't get a fair shake.

She proceeds to enlighten me.

Three men are standing at a fence trying to look over the top. One is almost able to see over, but not quite. One is five or six inches too short to see over. The third is quite small and has no hope to see over.

Equality gives them all the same size box to stand on. It's a four-inch-high box. Now the tallest man is able to see over easily. The middle guy can only see over on his tippy toes. The shortest guy still has no hope of seeing to the other side.

Justice gives all three men a box too. The tallest man gets a box two inches tall, the middle man gets a six-inch box, and the last man gets a box that is a foot tall. Now all three men have been elevated to the point that they all have the same view over the fence.

She goes on to explain that white American culture has been focusing on equality and doesn't realize that equality does not always make outcomes equal. But justice says, if you need more because you are at a greater disadvantage, I'll do more to help you out.

My daughter wants me to understand that while all men may be created equal, America needs to wake up to the fact that God didn't tell us in Micah 6:8 to do equally. He instructs us to do justice. It is required of us by our heavenly Father.

Yes, equity would be even better. If we could start over from the beginning; if we could have realized from the start that all men are created equally, then we may have had equity. Things would have been fair and impartial. God even instructs impartiality throughout Scripture.

In Galatians 3:28 (NKJV), we're told, "*There is neither Jew nor Greek, there is neither slave nor free, there is no male and female, for you are all one in Christ Jesus.*" This is all in reference to being called children of God, being in line for the blessings of Abraham's seed if we live for Christ. We all qualify. There is equity.

But we have wronged others. We are a nation built on the backs of slaves. We wronged the first people, the Native Americans. In these, and many more areas, we must now make things right. We must give justice where justice is due.

Love Mercy

> *"Mercy triumphs over judgment." James 2:13b (NKJV)*

> *"Blessed are the merciful, for they will receive mercy." Matthew 5:7 (NASB)*

Arthur Burk does an incredible deep dive on the redemptive gifts in his book that I mentioned earlier. If you have not gone through his study on the seven gifts from Romans 12—prophet, servant, teacher, exhorter, giver, ruler, and mercy—I highly recommend you do. I have used it as a tool to better serve my staff at work. It helps me to understand what drives them, what their struggles are, and how to communicate with them.

When our church did the study several years back, I went into it assuming I had a teacher gifting. Or maybe mercy. Or maybe ruler. Whatever my primary gifting was, I was sure of one thing: It most definitely was not prophet! Oh, ye of little knowledge.

To my shock, all my friends knew I had the prophet gifting. It was no surprise to them, but it was to me! I had misunderstood the gift; and I had misunderstood myself. But this study helped me embrace who God created me to be, and it brought great relief to my heart when I finally understood why I process things the way I do.

One defining characteristic of those with the prophet gifting is that we see things in black and white. There is no room for gray. And that outlook can be processed as judgmentalism in its immaturity.

A mature prophet (speaking of the gifting of prophet here, not the office of prophet) understands that there is grace for all and we are called to love all—as they are. There is no room for us to judge. It's not our job.

About thirty years ago, my then-husband and I lived in an apartment next door to a neighbor who was obviously a bit of a partier. It was during this time that I learned a difficult lesson on laying aside judgement and walking in humility.

Strange smells seeping through the walls between our apartments, young people of all ages coming and going from his unit, all pointed to a lifestyle being lived next door that I did not want any part of.

I did not know his name for months. I avoided his eyes so I wouldn't have to speak to him. I did not want to be neighborly to my "druggy" neighbor.

Then one morning, our upstairs neighbor told us that our next-door neighbor had been taken by ambulance in the night; apparently, an overdose of some unknown drugs. The kids that had been with him were too scared to admit that they knew what he took. No one would come forward to help the doctors. And word was that he was in bad shape.

It hit me hard. I lived right next door to a young man, not much older than me, who was struggling. And I did nothing for months. I was not friendly. I did not reach out in love.

We were able to find out a phone number for his parents, who lived out of state. They were Christians, and he was their Christian son who just a few years prior had gone through an unfair event that had cost him his career. The drugs were his way of coping with the disappointment and hopelessness. He had needed encouragement. I could have given him that. But I failed because I judged him.

Instead, we were granted permission to go to the hospital and pray over him. What we encountered there is something I had never seen before and hope to never see again.

If you've not seen what chemical destruction does to a dying body, I do not recommend it. It was difficult to look at him in his unconscious state. Fluids escaping from his swollen, off-colored body; and so very still and lifeless.

We stood together in prayer over him and spoke to his spirit, encouraging him. We let him know his parents were on the way. They did not make it in time.

Judgement did him no good. It did me no good. I was humbled.

Walk Humbly

> *"Call to me and I will answer you and tell you*
> *great and unsearchable things you do not know."*
> *Jeremiah 33:3 (NIV)*

The way forward is humility. This is a series that my pastor has been doing in the midst of the coronavirus pandemic. And it's a revelation I got from the Lord several years back.

As a child with low self-esteem, who grew into a young adult with low self-esteem, I considered myself a humble person.

But now that I have matured into a more informed under-standing of what humility is, I know that low self-esteem is actually the opposite of humility. It's actually quite self-centered. It is pride.

At some point in my adult life, I realized my need for humility. Because I was marred by ridicule and harsh words in my youth, I was cautious about appearing foolish to others. But when I realized I needed to be more vulnerable, I came up with a plan to learn humility. The plan began with animals and children.

It's really easy to talk to children and animals in cute, happy phrases: "Hello, pretty girl. What a beautiful girl you are." "Who's a good boy? You're a good boy." "You're a sweet baby, aren't you? Yes, you are." Nobody looks at you sideways when it concerns kids and pets.

So, that's where I started. I allowed myself to be humble in my interactions when I encountered children, babies, dogs, cats. It gave me an opportunity to not worry about what people thought of me. I could be silly and gush without fear of ridicule. And once I learned that skill, I moved on to other people.

I found that once I was able to lower myself to baby talk kids and animals, the next obvious step was saying kind things to the elderly and those in need. Then it got a little easier to serve others of various ages and types. The more I opened myself up to being humble, the easier it was to be humble; to make myself less to make others more important. I prayed for opportunities to serve others. I sent secret pal notes and small gifts to other ladies, just to see them smile. And the more I served, the more I embraced humility. But there was still a prideful stronghold that remained, keeping me from true humility—judgmentalism.

Learning Humility

It's taken many years for me to mature in this particular area. But I am learning daily to lay aside pride and walk in humility. I've learned to call on God, as instructed in Jeremiah 33:3, because there are things I do not know (so many things).

In 2014, following a twenty-year career as a technical writer/editor, and a short-lived stint running my own business, I was ready for a change. I was ready to follow my passion for horses and my desire to help people. I found a job posting for a therapeutic riding center that helps individuals with trauma and those with physical and cognitive needs find physical and mental help through equine. Perfect! Sign me up.

I interviewed for the job just days later, but as I left the interview, I knew within my spirit that I had not gotten the job;

though I also knew I had established an important connection with the CEO/founder of that nonprofit organization.

Over the next two-and-a-half years, she and I connected several times, trying each time to find what our professional relationship would be. Over that period of time, the desire to work together was there, but God had a plan for me before He would release me to do the good work I felt called to do.

His plan—teach me about humility.

In 2015, when my business closed due to non-payment of invoices by my biggest client, I was forced to find a job. The job that came was not the one I wanted. In fact, I did not want it at all. It grieved me tremendously to accept the position. It was a demotion, a huge step down. It was humiliating.

The stress of taking that job caused me to develop a case of shingles. My first day on the job, I was about a week into suffering with the horribly painful illness. But I did not let on. I suffered in silence. I could barely function, but I would not show my cards.

I cried. I cried a lot. I was in that job for nine months, and for the first four and a half months, I cried at my desk every day. Nobody knew. I was a good secret crier. I did productive work, even in misery—physically and emotionally.

One night, I had a dream. In the dream, I saw my childhood horse, Rooster. He was led into a big barn full of stalls. But instead of being put into an empty stall on the front row, where all the large, roomy, four-sided stalls were located, he was taken to the back row, back in the shadows where the stalls were smaller. And they weren't even full stalls. They were just three walls.

I cried foul! *What the heck? Why was Rooster being demoted to a lesser stall? Why wasn't he given a nicer, more prominent stall?*

The next morning, sitting in my cubicle, I looked over to the executive office across the hall from me. The glass walls displayed a big, roomy desk and beautiful décor. As I sat there looking at what just a year or two prior could have been my office, I heard the Lord speak.

He told me that I was Rooster. I was in the back-row, open-sided stall, while others occupied the four-walled, roomy stalls. But in His next words, He imparted such loving wisdom to me, I'll never forget His words.

"Kelli," He said, "Rooster was put in the small, open-sided stall because he could be trusted. The unruly horses were placed in the larger, enclosed stalls because they could not be trusted. It was not a demotion; it was a sign of trust." And I realized that God had not put me in the small, open-sided cubicle to punish me. He trusted me.

I was undone. I was humbled.

During this same time, God took me on a study of humility through the life of Moses. He showed me what it looks like to be a friend of God and to be called the most humble man on earth.

What a gracious God.

I believe I stayed at that job for nine months so that God could birth something new within me.

I have learned over the years that probably the most important characteristic of an effective leader is humility. And God had a plan for me to walk into a position of leadership where I would need this skill in my toolbelt. It was an expensive tool to acquire, but so worth having.

At the end of those nine months, I came on as the chief of staff at the therapeutic equestrian center, and now, five years later, I'm still there as chief of operations. I'm so thankful that God took time to equip me. It's earned me a place of honor and trust. And I am able to serve my organization well.

Back before God took me on the humility walk, I was constantly getting the numbers one, two, three, four. If you Google "What is the number for humility," your search will return Numbers 12:3. *"Now the man Moses was very humble, more than all men who were on the face of the earth."* (NKJV)

Just today, as I was driving to work, I saw a reminder of something I heard about humility just recently: humility + nothing = promotion. I looked down at the curb while I sat at a red light. This is what I saw.

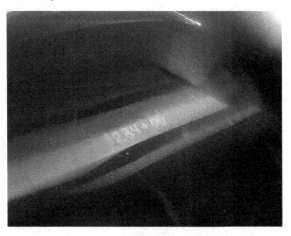

Humility + Nothing = Promotion

One final note on Moses: When God called him to confront Pharaoh and lead the nation of Israel, he argued with God that he was not a good speaker. Note: You might not be good (yet) at what God has called you to do. But humbly stepping out in faith is key.

The Field

In 2014, two years prior to starting work at the nonprofit equestrian organization, my pastor spoke a word over me. He said the Lord needed to move me out of where I was (job) and into something new. He said I had taken a step of faith, but where I was at that point in time was just part of a journey I was on. "This is not *it*," he said. "In the next twenty-one days, keep your ears open, and it will be revealed. It's something bigger. You're tracking toward a destination."

That something bigger was the walk of humility that ultimately led me to my current job.

During that same year, God began to speak to me in ways He never had before. And I began to gain understanding into the spirit world like I never had before. I am still amazed at some of the encounters that occurred starting in 2014 and continued strongly through 2018. The veil between heaven and earth was thin in that time.

Our pastor's good friend, Kent Mattox, came to preach a message at our church on December 8, 2014. I will never forget that message. It set off within me the timing of stepping into what God was calling me to, vocationally.

Pastor Kent told of how he and his wife planned a vacation to a dude ranch. But they then realized their need to learn to ride horses before leaving for that adventure. The horseback riding lessons they signed up for made them fall in love with horses. So, they bought one, then another, and ultimately ended up with thirteen. What do you do when you're a pastor with thirteen horses? You start a cowboy church.

As he told the story of his family's journey into horses, I wept. Tears just poured down my cheeks through the whole sermon. Something about his words touched something deep within me. I was meant to help people through horses.

Two and a half years later, the night before starting my new job at the therapeutic riding center, I had a dream. I saw a large, green pasture. And as I looked, a horse came thundering across the field, with a woman perched upon the horse's back, trick riding. I watched the woman in amazement. And I remember thinking that I could never ride a horse like that. I didn't have her talent. Then instantly in the dream, I heard God speak. "Kelli," He said. "This field is yours. I've called you to it. I haven't called you to ride like her. But the field is yours."

The next day, I started my new job. And that day, I learned that there were some exceptional horse women working for the organization. One of them was a trick rider, her equestrian skills far beyond my own. But I knew I was in the position I was called to. I had entered my *field of calling*.

March 2016, First Week on the New Job

Dreamer

I've always been a dreamer. And the things that God has whispered into my night ear and placed before my night eye over the years have been astounding. But only once in my life have I had an encounter like I had the night of December 15, 2014.

During that season, I had regularly been pressing in and seeking God at a depth like never before. And that night, shortly after I laid down to sleep, I was awakened. Sort of.

I can only explain it to be like a sleep-awake state. I was aware of my husband breathing deeply next to me. I could see my bedroom around me in the dark. But I was also very aware of another presence in the room. And though I was not looking at him, I knew the other presence was a gray-haired man with a beard. He stood to my left and placed his right arm around my back. Then very quickly he placed his right hand on the right side of my back, just below my shoulder blade. And with that quick touch, he placed a stamp on me. It was about the size of a dessert plate and square like a postage stamp. It was a marking.

I looked at the clock; it was 11:11. I still felt a presence in the room. I was a little afraid. The thought came to mind, *This is step one.* And then I fell back asleep.

Twelve minutes later, I awoke to look at the clock again: 11:23. This time I stayed awake a few minutes, still very aware of a presence in the room. I decided to trust God that it was a godly presence.

Several questions went through my mind. *How do I have courage for angelic encounters? How do I become bold? And what did the stamp, or branding, mean?*

Just then God told me to go back to sleep and He would reveal things.

Not long after that encounter, I read the following Scripture, and I knew it explained what had happened.

> *"Now it is God who makes both us and you stand firm in Christ. He anointed us, set his seal of ownership on us, and put his Spirit in our hearts*

as a deposit, guaranteeing what is to come."
(2 Cor. 1:21-22, NIV)

Do the Love Walk

A lot of writers have playlists they listen to while they write. I usually write in silence. But there is one song that I've played on loop for the past year—sometimes while writing, often while driving. It's *Jesus I Believe* by Big Daddy Weave.

This morning, I had it on loop on my drive into work. It was the first time I realized the opening line is key to the message of this book and particularly this chapter. I encourage you to listen to the song—it begins with the vocalist's desire to walk with Jesus and know He is near.

I want to walk with Jesus. I want to spend time with Him, getting to know Him better. Just like walks with my daughter or with a friend; it's an intimate, dedicated time of conversation.

When I was single, my friends and I went walking or running almost every day. It was great exercise, but it was also a time of exploring big questions, sharing deep concerns, giving godly revelation, etc. I cherish those memories of walking and talking with friends. Love walks.

What is a love walk?

The theme verse for this chapter is Micah 6:8. Micah is a minor prophet, meaning he is a prophet of the Old Testament that wrote a book that is relatively brief. But it is so rich.

Much of what Micah prophesized was directed toward Jerusalem. He spoke out against unjust leaders and defended the poor against the tyranny of the rich and powerful. He was a voice for justice.

In Micah 6:1-7, we see a rebuke against Israel for forgetting all that the Lord God had done for them. He brought them out of the slavery of Egypt. He sent them a leader in Moses, along with his brother, Aaron, and sister, Miriam. He saved them from the plot of Balak, the evil king of Moab.

Micah asks the Israelites, considering all that God has done for you, Israel, what does He require of you? Does He ask for a burnt offering of a year-old calf? Would He be pleased with thousands of rams or ten thousand rivers of olive oil? Maybe you should sacrifice your first-born child to atone for your sins. (I love Micah's sarcasm. He's my tribe.) "No," Micah says. "God has already told you what He requires of you (you bunch of big dummies...sorry, but I think it's implied.) Act justly. Love mercy. Walk humbly."

That's it.

Now obviously, since Jesus had not yet come and died to atone for mankind's sins, sacrifices were necessary. But what Micah is saying is, if you would just practice justice to people of all socioeconomic status, have merciful love for those around you, and walk out your life in humility, you wouldn't need to do anything else. You wouldn't need to bring sacrifices if you'd just live right.

John 15:13 (NIV) tells us, "*Greater love has no one than this: to lay down one's life for one's friends.*"

Jesus demonstrated this love walk on the road to Golgotha.

How can you do the love walk? Here are some ideas to get you started thinking. You might come up with other ideas or adapt some of these to suit your call to walk out love.

- Ask a friend to meet you for morning coffee to go. Walk, talk, and sip.
- Start a love walk small group with your pastor's blessing.
- Invite someone you know who is unchurched to go walking in the evenings. Get to know the person and find ways to demonstrate practical love to him or her.
- Take a walk through your community and look for things you can do to show love—pick up trash, help

pull an elderly neighbor's recycling bin to the curb,
walk your neighbor's dog.

- Plan a love walk-a-thon. Have people sign up and
  raise money to bless a worthy cause.

Whatever you do, find a way
to do justice, love mercy, walk
humbly. Do the love walk.

*Whatever you
do, find a way
to do justice,
love mercy, walk
humbly. Do the
love walk.*

CHAPTER 7:

God Speaks

❧❦❧

"In a dream, a vision of the night, when sound sleep
falls on men, while they slumber in their beds, then
He opens the ears of men, and seals their instruction."
Job 33:15-16 (NASB)

THE ONE THING I know for sure is that God is not
silent about His love for you, His plans for you, and
how you will reach your destiny. You just need an ear to hear.

For me, God has spoken in various ways—through dreams,
visions, numbers, signs, words, etc. I mentioned in the
last chapter that there was a season when I was seeing

and hearing "one, two, three, four" over and over. I'll talk about that a little more. But essentially, numbers can point to a time or a Scripture, or the numbers may be calling your attention so that you notice what is going on at that moment, either physically or spiritually. This is very biblical, as God consistently uses purposeful numbers throughout Scripture.

For example, the number forty. Jesus was tempted in the wilderness for forty days. Jesus, Moses, and Elijah all fasted forty days as well. There were forty days between the resurrection and ascension of Jesus. The Israelites wandered the desert for forty years. Moses was on Mount Sinai, where he received the Ten Commandments, for forty days. In Genesis, we read that God flooded the earth for forty days, and then Noah and his family sat on top of the mountains for forty days before releasing a raven. Goliath taunted the Israelites for forty days before David defeated him. And when the spies went into Canaan to check things out, they were there for forty days. So, it would seem that the number forty has a meaning related to a probationary time, or a time of testing and tribulation.

If you feel that you're called to attention, or a string of numbers seems to leap out at you, it's quite possible it's God saying something.

I really try to keep my spirit alert to the Holy Spirit through prayer, fasting, worship, and the Word so that I'm aware when God speaks in various ways. And sometimes, I'm amazed at what He shares.

On September 27, 2015, right after Yom Kippur, there was a blood moon. Just as I was awakening that morning, I looked over to the digital clock by my bed. And for a millisecond, as my eyes were opening, the digital numbers on the clock spelled out the word "SECRETS."

Nine days later, and in the two days after that, I came to understand the meaning of that vision.

It was October 6, 2015. I was at work making notes in a journal when, without thought, I doodled a drawing of an egg. And in the center of the egg, I wrote Golden Egg.

The next day, October 7, 2015, I felt like God was pointing out the number seven. He had actually been pointing it out for some time. So, when I arrived at work, I looked up the meaning of the number seven and came up with something I'd never read before.

October 7, 3761 BC, is the date according to Jewish tradition that God created Adam. (Green)

It struck me as important that on the day of October 7, 5776, I discovered this piece of information about the Hebrew date October 7, 3761. The aligning of October 7th was not lost on me. So, I dug deeper.

An unction within me said to subtract the first year, the Hebraic year 3761, from the current year, the Hebraic year 5776. So, I did. That's 5776 minus 3761. To my amazement, 5776 – 3761 = 2015! Subtracting the current Hebrew year from the first year of man's creation results in the current Gregorian year! I tried it over and over, and discovered that it works for every Gregorian year in the final three months of the calendar year—October 7th to December 31st.

To this day, I do not have an understanding of the true meaning of this or why God showed it to me. Perhaps other people already knew about it, but it was all new to me. I think that it has to do with man coming into alignment with God, but I still await a deeper understanding.

That's how it is many times with what God reveals. It must be unpacked. It needs additional pieces at another time. Many times, it's a journey to discover revelation.

Now, what about that little "Golden Egg" I had doodled the day before? Stay with me. It gets even more interesting.

The same morning that I got the revelation about the dates, I had a dream I'll never forget.

I had awakened around 4:30 that morning, processing another dream, when I drifted back into a light sleep and began to dream again. In this dream, I saw the date January 2012. Then I heard the prophet Bob Jones speaking from heaven, standing in a garden. And I thought he said to me, "CCLOT," or "CLOT." I could both see and hear the word he released to me, but I was unsure of exactly what the word was.

So, later that day, I did a search on "Bob Jones' prophecy for January 2012." And I found that he had released a word about January 2012. It was a word called *Peace, Prosperity, & the Returning Glory!* (Jones)

In that word, he tells of being on a train—the glory train—with many other shepherds. The conductor handed him a time capsule; and it was shaped like an egg! The egg had new life in it. It contained the beginning and end of time. Bob asked the conductor, "When can I open this egg, and when will this train arrive?" (He had the dream in September 2009.) The conductor said the time was within the egg and the egg will be opened in 2012.

The egg! I had drawn the golden egg just the day before. And I had dreamt January 2012 and seen Bob Jones that very night. And then it occurred to me; God had given me the insight to the SECRETS. The revelation was about the beginning and ending of time. It was about 5776 – 3761 = 2015.

The next night, October 8, 2015, I dreamt again. In this dream, I visited a farm and I carried a satchel. Within my bag, I had two items to share with others—a peacock feather and an egg. In the dream, when I went to show the items to people at work, the egg was a broken-open shell.

Peacock feathers have a pattern that looks like an eye on their tip. This often represents eyes to see. And the broken-open egg, I believe, ties to the egg-shaped time capsule given to Bob Jones. The conductor told him the egg would be opened in 2012.

With all of this in mind, I looked at the dream again where I had met Bob Jones and he had released a word. I believe the word was not "CLOT" or "CCLOT," but it was "CLOCK," in reference to "SECRETS" on the face of my clock.

> *"Surely the Lord God does nothing, unless He*
> *reveals His secret to His servants the prophets."*
> *Amos 3:7 (NKJV)*

"It is the glory of God to conceal a matter, but the glory of kings is to search out a matter." Proverbs 25:2 (NKJV)

It is this type of revelation that I regularly write down in my journal. Over time, I'm drawn back as new revelation is revealed; and the revelation continues to unfold. Often, it reveals something about me or the path I'm on. Sometimes, it points to areas I need to pray into. Occasionally, it's a heads-up for someone else. Rarely is it literal.

I hear from God through dreams, in things I see, through numbers, in messages from others, and a dozen other ways. Often, I understand the meaning immediately. Sometimes, I have to search it out. I always pray, I always seek, to make sure I am on track. When I don't get anything in the way of interpretation, I let it sit in my journal until it's called back up, like the Bob Jones dream.

Two years ago, I was driving to work listening to a friend's podcast on writing a book. Suddenly, a recurring word came to me—Title Nine.

Now if you don't know what Title Nine is, it's actually Title IX, and it's a federal civil rights law that was passed in 1972. And it says, "No person in the United States shall, based on sex, be excluded from participation in, be denied the benefits of, or be subjected to discrimination under any education program or activity receiving Federal financial assistance." (Title IX)

This law was a follow-up to the Civil Rights Act of 1964 that was passed to end discrimination based on race, color, religion, sex, or national origin when it comes to employment and public accommodation. But it failed to address this for anyone employed by an educational institution.

Title VI was passed to prohibit discrimination in federally funded private and public entities, but the wording left out sex and only addressed race, color, religion, and national origin.

In the 1970s, feminists lobbied Congress to add sex in as a protected class—which resulted in Title IX for federally funded education programs, thereby protecting the rights of women in this area.

That day last December when Title Nine popped into my head, it was not the first time it had come to me. I had gotten it several times over the previous year. But this time, as it popped into my head, I began saying it over and over to myself, and as I said it, my cadence and volume increased. Title Nine. Title Nine. Title Nine! The title is Nine! Suddenly, I realized that it was a title. Was it the title of a book? Was it the title of my book? Immediately, I looked at my dashboard and the time and temperature read, "7:14 66°." My birthday—7/14/66. God was confirming.

Turns out it was a word for another time. It set me on a journey to write this book, but it is only in finishing this one that I realized my next book has a significant reason for having "nine" in the title. I can't wait to get started on it.

In 2018, the year before I got "the title is Nine," I was driving to work behind a van that belonged to a carpet-cleaning business. I had been getting the word "victory" a lot in that season. So, the company name on the carpet-cleaning van, Victorious, caught my eye. I noticed that their phone number was 407-777-1418. Immediately, it hit me that the number sequence was forty years of the Israelites wandering in the desert, followed by 777, and then my birthday that year—7/14/18. It was an encouragement to me that God saw me and wanted me to get the victory.

These are just examples of how I hear from God. He speaks quietly, in parables. You have to lean in; you have to be humble; you have to be expectant to see and hear Him consistently.

This happened another time that same year. I was driving home from a business trip to the coast, and I was asking God what my purpose and calling were. Immediately, I passed two billboards. One had an advertisement that said, "You have a role to play." The other was an ad for Wonderworks. In my mind, I heard, "Signs and wonders." And I knew God had a kingdom purpose for my life. I had a role to play in signs and wonders.

I mentioned before that there was a period of time that I was getting "one, two, three, four" all the time. I'd look at a clock just in time to see it as 12:34, or it would show up in the oddest places.

One day, I stopped at a Publix grocery store to buy some birthday bakery treats for a friend. The clerk boxed my purchase and printed the price sticker. As she handed it to me, the price caught my eye. I'd only bought about $4.00 of baked goods, but the sticker read $12.34. When I questioned her, she replied, "Yeah, I don't know why that printed." To which I responded, "I know why." God was speaking, drawing my attention to something. I still have that price sticker in my journal.

That same year, we did a twenty-one-day fast, and on day one, we had a power surge that took out our electricity. When I looked at the phone later, I saw that my husband had called the power company at 12:34. My attention was drawn to the "power" of fasting. We were on track; it was confirmed.

I'll mention one other significant "one, two, three, four" that happened that same year.

I had a meeting with the CEO of the organization where I now work. But at that time, it was just a meeting to see if there was a way forward for us to work together. It was one of the many meetings we had during my two and a half years of job interviews with her. (Patience is a virtue.) She shared with me how over the years she had hired people and it just didn't work out. Then she shared something that made my jaw drop. She said that often times after several attempts of finding a good employee fit, "one, two, three, four, and you hire the right person."

I had to tell her how God had been sending me "one, two, three, four" words. That led to a discussion on our mutual belief in the ways God speaks. And as it turns out, "one, two, three, four," she did hire the right person. Me!

God doesn't just talk to us when big things, like job changes, are happening. He's into our small details too.

I'm being really transparent here.

God doesn't just talk to us when big things, like job changes, are happening. He's into our small details too.

I love corporate worship. And often, I get really deep into it: hands up, eyes closed, communing with the Lord. When suddenly, a tap on my shoulder, and I'm jolted back to earth, eyes wide open. Someone has shown up late to church and would like me to step out and let him or her into my row.

I have to tell you. I come right out of God's glory and go right into thinking mean thoughts. Be on time, people! Show some respect for worship people! (Just being real here.)

So, a few years ago, I was getting my worship on and suddenly God says to me, "Some people are coming who will want to come into your row. But don't worry. You'll not leave my presence."

About eight seconds later, two ladies are squeezing in behind me, and I have to step out of the way. Well, guess what?! I stepped back into my spot, put my hands back up, and instantly I was right back in worship in God's presence. It was awesome!

God knew my weakness. And He really wanted me to have victory over it. So, He spoke into the situation and gave direction. I love it!

Heads-up, words can be incredible. But sometimes, they are preparing us for a difficulty coming our way. God gave me a heads-up several years back that I'd be losing one of my pets.

I've always had cats; some have been more special than others for one reason or another. Phin was an incredibly special cat. We just had a bond.

One night, I had a dream that I was carrying Phin in a crowd of people outside a set of very tall, elaborate gates. I could hear a horse race being called in the distance. At one point in the dream, I looked at Phin in my arms and told him I was so glad I had brought him. Then I put Phin down outside those gates.

It was just twenty days after that dream that we discovered a large tumor had grown in Phin's throat. Within days, we had to put him down.

In the dream, "putting him down" meant setting him down. But those play-on words were a heads-up that I'd be saying goodbye to my buddy in a matter of weeks. The elaborate gates seem to have been the "pearly gates."

I mourned that cat. Some days, the grief would wash over me. I was having a difficult day a couple weeks after he died. And I looked out my office window to where his grave was and saw that the yard was filled with birds—red birds, blue birds, finch, a woodpecker, and, on the fence behind his grave, were two peace doves. Those doves did not move from that spot for four hours. It was so comforting to see them there. And it was even more special that there were two of them, as buried right next to Phin was our cat Dusty, who had died just days before we had to put Phin down.

I could go on and on about the different ways and times God has revealed things to me, or sent words, or pointed something out. It's all part of discovering who I am and what I'm called to be. And if you take an inventory, you'll see a picture emerging too.

God created you to be you for His good glory. Taking practical steps can help you discover your calling and who you are created to be. You can start by asking yourself these nine questions and honestly answering them.

1. What do you like or need to make you happy?
2. What have you always wanted to do?
3. What do you believe you do well?
4. What do other people tell you you're good at?
5. What do you not like or what's not important to you?
6. What types of resistance have you encountered?
7. What would you do if money was no object?
8. What has God said?
9. What have you done to purse your calling?

For my own personal walk, I'm sure there will be some surprises along the way. And I'll probably lose faith in the process now and then, but I think that's why I love my "writing song," "Jesus I Believe" by Big Daddy Weave. I have listened to it on loop for the entirety of writing this book.

The final two stanzas of this song reference the story found in Mark 9. A man's son has a mute spirit that tortures him. The father asks the disciples to help, but they are unable to cast out the spirit. So, he comes to Jesus for help.

In verse 23 (NKJV), Jesus says to him, "*If you can believe, all things are possible to him who believes.*"

To which the father replies in verse 24 (NKJV), "*Lord, I believe; help my unbelief!*"

I love this verse. The man desperately wants the faith to believe for his son's healing. He yells out—"I believe!" But, in his humanness, he confesses he is weak. He lacks faith. Help me believe, Lord.

Jesus, I do believe. Help me, God. Help me to live the destiny You put within me. Help me to live out Your mission for me. Help me to walk in the fields You've led me to—my fields of calling. I know You'll lead me, Holy Spirit. I know You'll use me, even in my weakness. I believe You've called me. I believe You've equipped me. Jesus, I believe.

Acknowledgements

T HE LOVE OF writing has always been present in my life. In grade school, I thought myself a short-story writer and poet. In college, I imagined *National Geographic* would be waiting to the side of the tassel-turning stage, ready to whisk me off to Africa where I'd pen the plight of the Rothschild's giraffe or the mountain gorilla. Instead, twenty years of user guides, technical manuals, and master plans were my vocation. I learned though. I learned how to write and how to edit. But I also learned to inter-view; to collaborate; to have patience; and to be authentic, humble, and kind. Twenty-one years more, and the world-wide COVID-19 pandemic hit. And God said, "You've got time now. Write a book." In fact, He spoke a Scripture to me: Jeremiah 30:2 (AMP). "*Thus says the Lord God of Israel, 'Write in a book all the words which I have spoken to you.'*"

Four months of really early mornings, late nights, and full weekends later, and the bulk of this book was penned. It took a "divine pause" for me to do what God had called me to do. And it is to God, first and foremost, that I must give acknowledgement.

My walk and friendship with my Savior has been lifelong, but there is still so far to go and so much more to know. I come to the garden alone, while the dew is still on the roses—daily. It's these special times with Him that sustain me. It's where I get my marching orders. Time; there is no replacement for that.

And then, there are so many people to acknowledge for what you read in this book. So many family, friends, leaders, co-workers who have affected my life and said or done things that they may not realize left an impression on me. I could never name them all.

I must acknowledge my family. I am so grateful to have been raised by godly parents, Jim and Faye. They have always been sources of strength, encouragement, and faith for my three siblings and me: Kathy, Lori, and Keith. Thank you, family. I love you. And to my husband, Chris, and my three living children, Nicole, Lexie, and Shane—you make my world go round. I have no greater joy than to walk this road with you. You have all my love. And to my heavenly baby, Alex: I can't wait to sit and chat forever. Your memory is a bright spot.

Next, I want to recognize my many dear friends at Thrive Church Apopka. This place—it's my "dinner spot." Pastor Kevin feeds us the revelatory meat of the Word, and it is so refreshing and life-sustaining. Thank you, PK. And of course, many thanks also go to our pastor's support system, AKA his wife and my friend. Kelly, thank you. And thank you to the ladies at the other end of the line: Vickie, Hillary, Laura, and Megan. You're always there, with wisdom, with wit, and with open arms.

Then there's the women of McCormick and our leader, Thomasa. I love working shoulder-to-shoulder with you all as we show the world how special horses are.

So many more special people...how do I thank and recognize you all?!

Finally, being the horse-lover that I am, I must acknowledge all the lovely beasts who've taught me and been there for me, from my first horse, Rooster, to my current little mini buddy, Hank. Horses are awesome, and you all have been the best.

To all, I am grateful.

Works Cited

1. Arnold, Samuel. "Humpty Dumpty." Juvenile Amusements, 1797.
2. Burk, Arthur A. *The Redemptive Gifts of Individuals*. Plumbline Ministries, 2000.
3. Chapman, Gary. *The 5 Love Languages*. Northfield Publishing, 2015.
4. Geurs, Karl. *Pooh's Grand Adventure: The Search for Christopher Robin*. Walt Disney World Television Animation, 1997.
5. Green, David B. "This Day in Jewish History." *Haaretz*, 1 Oct. 2015, www.haaretz.com/jewish/3761-bce-the-world-is-created-1.5405777.

6. Goll, James W. "Hope in Front of You with Danny Gokey," from *God Encounters Today Podcast*, June 30, 2020, https://godencounterstoday.libsyn.com/finding-hope-in-your-darkest-moments-with-danny-gokey-season-2-ep-30.

7. Jones, Bob. "*Peace, Prosperity, & the Returning Glory!*" from *Did You Learn to Love?* September 2009, http://didyoulearntolove.org/2012/01/03/peace-prosperity-the-returning-glory/.

8. Lewis, C.S. *Voyage of the Dawn Treader.* 1950, Geoffrey Bles.

9. "Miklat." *International Fellowship of Christians and Jews*, 13 May 2020, www.ifcj.org/learn/learn-hebrew/hwod/miklat.

10. Popik, Barry, et al. "Choose a Job You Love, and You Will Never Have to Work a Day in Your Life." *Quote Investigator*, 3 Jan. 2019, quoteinvestigator.com/2014/09/02/job-love.

11. "Title IX." *Wikipedia*, 23, May 2021, en.wikipedia.org/wiki/Title_IX.

About the Author

❧

THE CHIEF OPERATIONS officer at McCormick Research Institute, a nonprofit equine-assisted services organization, Kelli Pharo has over thirty years' experience in writing, communication, and leadership, and a lifetime of experience in horses. Her call to help people through horses and to use her writing talent to serve God resulted in this book. Kelli shares her own path to discovering her fields of calling in order to help others do the same. Kelli, her husband, Chris, and two of their children live in Central Florida.

CPSIA information can be obtained
at www.ICGtesting.com
Printed in the USA
BVHW041432080721
611455BV00013B/1185